SALVATION THROUGH SEX
The Life and Work
of Wilhelm Reich

Morrow Books by Eustace Chesser

STRANGE LOVES:
The Human Aspects of Sexual Deviation

SALVATION THROUGH SEX:
The Life and Work of Wilhelm Reich

SALVATION THROUGH SEX
The Life and Work of Wilhelm Reich

by Eustace Chesser

William Morrow & Company, Inc., New York 1973

Published in the United States in 1973.
Copyright © 1972 by Eustace Chesser
Published in Great Britain in 1972 under the title
Reich and Sexual Freedom.

Printed in the United States of America
Library of Congress Catalog Card Number 73-9355

ISBN 0-688-00182-3

1 2 3 4 5 75 74 73

To D.A.

Table of Contents

SALVATION
THROUGH SEX
The Life and Work
of Wilhelm Reich

1 The Tormented Genius

Wilhelm Reich blazed the trail which led, after his tragic death, to what is now known as the Permissive Society. That is why in the Underground Press and among the younger generation in revolt against the Establishment the name of Reich is honoured today, whereas most of the other early disciples of Freud are either ignored or forgotten. For Reich, too, rebelled against the Establishment. In the end it killed him and with a bureaucratic blindness ordered his books and papers to be destroyed. Yet the message Reich tirelessly preached, except in the last years when the strain of a lifetime of persecution took its toll, was "Make love, not war". And if that sounds strangely contemporary it is because Reich's theories and outlook were fifty years ahead of his time.

He was a pioneer of sex education and this led to a lifelong friendship with A. S. Neill of Summerhill school. *The Little Red Schoolbook*, which was the subject of a prosecution in 1971, is a not specially bold application of Reich's view that sexual freedom should begin at puberty. He was deeply impressed by Malinowski's study of the sexual customs of the Trobriand Islanders, who began to have intercourse as soon as they were physically capable, with complete social approval. Malinowski became one of Reich's closest friends.

As a psychiatrist Reich's most striking contribution lay in his psychosomatic approach. His use of oscillographs to record the response to pleasure ante-dated the experiments of Masters and Johnson. It would have been unthinkable at that time to have recorded an orgasm, but Reich undoubtedly pointed the way to the sex laboratory.

He believed that the key to neurotic problems could be found in the body, not in the mind. He denied, of course, that body

7

and mind were separate entities. Whereas orthodox psychoanalysis tried to dredge repressed material by getting the patient to talk, Reich concentrated on re-educating the patient's posture and muscles. An actual physical blockage had to be removed before total satisfaction could be achieved in sex.

A more daring speculation was that the term "libido", or sexual energy, had a positive measurable, physical aspect. He was convinced in the latter part of his life that he had discovered a new fundamental factor in Nature which he called "orgone". Many who welcomed his psychoanalytic theories found it impossible to follow him in these flights. His enemies said he was mad.

Many brilliant men have been thought deranged because they did not conform to the ideas of their time. Genius, however, is more often allied to crankiness than to madness. Newton laid the foundations of modern physics and invented the calculus before he was twenty-five; thereafter he devoted his life to studying the prophecies of the book of Daniel, but no one said he was mad.

The Young Rebel

Wilhelm Reich was born in Galicia in 1897, the son of Jewish parents who became assimilated. He idolized his mother and suffered a severe trauma when she committed suicide. He feared that he had been unwittingly responsible in revealing her love affair with one of his tutors. His attitude to his father may be judged from his belief that he was not really his father's son.

After serving in the Austrian Army in the First World War, Reich studied medicine in Vienna. When he qualified he worked at first as an assistant in the psychiatric clinic of Julius Wagner-Jauregg. He was already happily married to Annie Pink, a fellow medical student who also became a psychoanalyst.

The decade after the First World War was dominated by two systems of thought, Communism and Psychoanalysis. Both were fashionable in Vienna and they did not seem so incompatible as they came to appear later. Reich set himself the task of reconciling Marx and Freud.

Like so many other intellectuals who had lived through defeat in war and struggled with property he looked upon the Russian Revolution as a glorious liberation. He felt like the young Wordsworth at the time of the French Revolution : "Bliss was it in that dawn to be alive,/But to be young was very heaven!"

Marx was right, and so was Freud : but how could their great discoveries be used to help the mass of people? He joined the Austrian Socialist Party and became clinical assistant at Freud's Psychoanalytic Polyclinic, which brought him into closer contact with the working class. He was anxious to place knowledge of sexual hygiene within reach of industrial workers and so remove the reproach that psychoanalysis was a middle-class luxury. Five years later he opened the first sex hygiene clinic which provided free information on birth control, child-rearing and sex education. This may not seen very revolutionary to us today, but it was otherwise in Vienna in 1929; and in England at the same time Marie Stopes was fighting a lone battle against bigotry and prejudice to achieve a similar object.

It was inevitable that his political interests should bring Reich gradually to question the neutral attitude required of strictly Freudian analysts. He also broke away from the orthodox line even while he was the director of a training institute for analysts from 1924–30. This was one of the most creative periods of his life. In 1927 his book *The Function of the Orgasm* was brought out by the International Psychoanalytic Publishing House, and in 1928 he published a paper on *Character Analysis* which was subsequently elaborated into a book. Many still think this was his most important contribution.

Dr. Charles Rycroft, for example, in a fiercely critical and often contemptuous study of Reich nevertheless pays tribute to his work in the Seminar for Psychoanalytic Therapy. "It should be mentioned here that Reich contributed significantly to the developments of psychoanalysis which transformed it from what in retrospect appears as an amateurish activity into a professional technique that can be taught formally." (*Reich* by Charles Rycroft, Fontana/Collins, 1971.)

After this acknowledgment it is extraordinary that Dr. Rycroft should describe Reich's life as 'tormented, persecuted and

9

futile". His attitude is characteristic of the treatment which Reich received all through his stormy career.

Sex and Politics

At first Freud treated Reich's theory that all neurosis can be traced to unfulfilled sex with a somewhat patronizing tolerance. He called it Reich's hobby-horse. But when Reich asked Freud to give him personal analysis he refused, ostensibly on the grounds that he had a rule not to accept anyone belonging to his close circle. It should be remembered that in those early years, when psychoanalysis was still developing its techniques, it was not yet obligatory for all analysts to be analysed.

Reich's social conscience made him impatient of the narrowly personal approach of Freud. He was opposed, too, to Freud's political pessimism. His own boundless energy found an outlet in the Communist Party which he joined in 1928. He believed with Marx that the task of philosophy was not merely to interpret the world but to change it.

From 1917–27 the Soviet Union had instituted a number of liberal laws on marriage, divorce, abortion and homosexuality. Reich went to Moscow in 1929 confidently expecting to find a new era. What was new, however, was not altogether to his liking. The Russians were more concerned with economics and the material standard of living than with sexual questions. Already a reaction from the early permissiveness had begun to set in.

The publication of *Dialectical Materialism and Psychoanalysis* in Moscow did not lead to a rapprochement between Marxism and Freudianism. On the contrary, it made both sides more conscious of their differences. In the end the rupture was complete and Reich was disowned by both. But he was still a party member when he moved to Berlin in 1930. Arthur Koestler, in *The God that Failed*, mentioned that he and Reich belonged to the same cell. "Among other members of our cell," Koestler writes, "I remember Dr. Wilhelm Reich, founder and director of Sex-Pol (Institute for Sexual Politics). He was a Freudian Marxist; inspired by Malinowski he had just published a book called *The Function of the Orgasm* in which he expounded the theory that the sexual frustration of the Proletariat caused a thwarting of its political consciousness; only through a full and uninhibited release of the sexual urge could the working class realize its revolutionary potentialities and historic mission; the whole thing was less cock-eyed than it sounds."

So far from being "cock-eyed" the programme of the German Association for Proletarian Sexual Politics, which had a membership of over 20,000, was so sane and sensible that most of the objectives have since been attained. The aims of the Association were :

(1) Better housing for the masses.
(2) Abolition of laws against abortion and homosexuality.
(3) Reform of marriage and divorce laws.
(4) Free birth control advice and contraception.
(5) Health protection for mothers and children.
(6) Nurseries in factories and other working centres.
(7) Abolition of laws prohibiting sex education.
(8) Home leave for prisoners.

That these items should have seemed dangerous and revolutionary in 1930 only shows how far we have moved since, and how many of Reich's ideas are now virtually taken for granted. He was passionately concerned to enable the mass of people to lead fuller lives. Unfortunately the means he advocated were repudiated by the two movements he had tried to bring together. The German Psychoanalytic Society asked him to resign in 1933. It may well be that under the growing shadow of the Swastika Reich's Communist affiliations were also an embarrassment.

Exile in Scandinavia

After publishing *The Mass Psychology of Fascism* he left Berlin for Vienna, but the Communists were not grateful. They felt, perhaps, that the rise of Hitler made Sexual Politics irrelevant, though Reich strongly disagreed. He was expelled from the Party and his books were withdrawn from Communist bookstalls. In Moscow his writings were dismissed as "un-Marxist rubbish".

Nor was this the only blow. His family life had disintegrated and in 1934 he was squeezed out of the International Psychoanalytical Association. The details of this manœuvre are obscure and do not sound very creditable.

This was the beginning of a series of persecutions which undoubtedly embittered him, though he never once swerved from the task he had set himself. He did not find the atmosphere in Vienna congenial, partly because of his Leftist associations, but mainly, perhaps, because Freud had formally declared that Reich was not suited to be a teaching analyst. This was virtual excommunication.

On the advice of a director of the World League for Sexual Reform he planned to settle in Denmark. There he was joined by Elsa Lindenberg, a ballet dancer he had met in Berlin. She strongly supported his political views, and the theories he was developing about the role of the musculature influenced her work as a teacher and choreographer of ballet. But the sojourn in Denmark which began so promisingly was brought to an end after six months when the Government revoked his permit to stay.

Where next could he find a refuge in which he could pursue his researches? Hopefully he visited England and met Malinowski. This was the start of his long friendship with the famous anthropologist. But Malinowski's theories clashed with the Freudian views on anthropology and Reich met with a cool reception by Ernest Jones and other psychoanalysts. Since he was not encouraged to stay in London, and now that Denmark, Germany and Austria were closed to him, he turned to Sweden. This provided only a brief respite. Once again his permit of sojourn was revoked after a short time.

By now he had gathered a band of enthusiastic analysts who were ready enough to defy the official ban. He was urged by this Scandinavian group to move to Norway. He was invited to give a series of lectures at the University of Oslo, and facilities were provided to carry out experiments on the electrical measurement of bodily stimulation. It really seemed as though he had found a haven at last.

For the next few years he worked happily on developing his theory of character analysis into what was at first called vegeto-therapy. Such a totally psychosomatic approach meant a final rupture with official psychoanalysis. The orthodox analyst adopts a stance of neutrality and never physically touches his patient. Reich, on the contrary, provoked the patient, clad in a swimsuit, to contract certain muscles and so become aware of which contractions were chronic.

"It is as a pioneer in the field of character analysis that Reich is most likely to be remembered," writes Dr. J. A. C. Brown, "for it was he who noted that reactive character traits were an armour used by the ego to protect it against both instincts and a thwarting environment. Such character traits as ambitious behaviour, which covers inadequacy, or arrogance, which hides deep feelings of inadequacy, do indeed protect the ego, but they have the serious defect that they are maintained indiscriminately, regardless of their appropriateness in a given situation and, because they insulate the individual from external stimuli, he becomes less susceptible to re-education." (*Freud and the Post-Freudians*, Penguin Books, 1961, p. 99.)

The way we stand, sit, walk give important clues to the character of a person. What he might tell an analyst, even in free association, could be deceptive. But the body does not lie. The drooping mouth, rigid abdomen, limp handshake reflect emotional states. Above all, if abdominal muscles are seized up by deep-rooted anxiety it is impossible for the body to respond freely and spontaneously during sexual intercourse.

Reich founded the International Instiute for Sex-Economy in 1936 to study the way the body uses its sexual energy. He concluded that this is largely determined by the type of society in which an individual is brought up. A patriarchal, authoritarian structure could be emotionally crippling. This aspect of Reich's work attracted the attention of A. S. Neill who joined the Institute and was trained in vegetotherapy.

Among the psychoanalysts who supported Reich at this stage and ignored the disapproval of the psychoanalytical establishment were Dr. Ola Raknes and Dr. Nic Waal. The latter specialized in child psychiatry and established an Institute in Oslo for treating disturbed children which still flourishes. But she was unable to follow Reich's biophysical speculations. These went beyond the usual frontiers of psychiatry. Reich now believed that the kind of pulsation that could be found in man—tension, charge, discharge, relaxation—occurred also in the lowest form of life. He spent part of his time in his Oslo laboratory where he observed the behaviour of protozoa and filmed them with a slow-motion camera.

He was driven on, despite the scepticism and even hostility of some who watched him, by a vision of the unity of life. The concept of energy was the unifying principle, but he did not use the term in a vague metaphorical sense, or to connate an imperceptible *élan vital* or life-force. By energy he meant an actual, physical ingredient in the universe which could be measured and harnessed. The pursuit of this idea became an obsession in the final phase of his life. Oslo and vegetotherapy belong to the middle period.

His biophysical research alienated Reich from a number of Norwegian psychiatrists and biologists and gave an opportunity for a pack of political opponents to harass him, hoping no doubt to drive him from Norway as he had been forced to flee from other countries. Between September 1937 and November 1938 a calumnious campaign was mounted against him in the Norwegian Press. Altogether over a hundred newspaper articles appeared. He was charged with distorting Malinowski's theories, which Malinowski promptly denied, and even accused of having had no training in psychoanalysis and not being a medical doctor. Palpable falsehoods mingled with scurrilous abuse. Leading newspapers referred to "the Jewish pornographer" and declared "God Reich creates life".

Dr. Theodore P. Wolfe, an Associate of Psychiatry in Columbia University, who subsequently translated some of Reich's books, advised Reich to emigrate to the United States. This he did in 1939, though it meant breaking with Elsa Lindenberg. He reached New York a few days before the outbreak of war in Europe.

The Discovery of Orgone

Soon after his arrival in America Reich married again. He set up the Orgone Institute, a laboratory and later a hospital at Forest Hills, Long Island. Despite the heavy setbacks he had suffered he was resilient and optimistic about the future. He was now convinced that he had made a scientific discovery, comparable to the Copernican Revolution. He had found a new kind of energy which could be stored in accumulators and used to strengthen the body against disease. He denied that he had claimed to cure disease, but it was inevitable that this was what the layman would conclude.

He was so confident of his laboratory results that he obtained an interview with Einstein. He persuaded Einstein to study his findings and look through an orgonoscope, an instrument he had invented to observe orgone energy in action. Einstein was friendly but unimpressed. The dream of enlisting the aid of the great physicist, and so winning the accolade of scientific respectability, came to nothing.

Reich now made two mistakes for which he was to pay dearly. He refused to undergo the formality of an examination which would have given him the legal right to practise medicine in the United States. What proved to be still more serious was the treatment of cancer patients by using cabinets, rather like narrow telephone boxes, which were said to be charged with orgone. Small boxes for home use to speed up the healing of wounds were also manufactured.

Reich became a United States citizen in 1946. By then he had founded the Orgone Institute Press in Greenwich Village, which enabled him to publish a Bulletin as well as papers and books. There was no doubt about the widespread interest aroused in his work, though it was not always of the kind he wanted.

The rumour spread, for example, that Orgone Accumulators could restore waning potency. This, together with the attacks in the Press that had begun again, only confirmed his view that the majority of people suffered from sexual failure. An article in *Harper's Magazine* entitled "The New Cult of Sex and Anarchy" was followed by a similar distortion in the *New Repub-*

15

lic headed "The Strange Case of Wilhelm Reich". History seemed to be repeating itself.

Reich had coined the term "emotional plague" for irrational actions in personal and social relationships which were derived from sexual frustration and frequently took the form of moralistic rigour. The "plague" was a disease of modern society. It was spread by religion, a belief which accounted for Reich's hostility to all religion. He held that a happy life for the majority of mankind is impossible unless the power of religion is broken. The importance of his analysis of religious psychology has been obscured by the more sensational aspects of his work. Yet his denunciation of "the mystical infestation of the masses" is integral to his outlook.

Government Investigations

One ominous result of the attacks in 1947 was the sudden interest taken in Orgone Therapy by the Food and Drug Administration. Designed to protect the public against dangerous quacks and sheer frauds the F.D.A. is a highly reputable organization. It was not concerned with the theoretical side of Reich's work, but Orgone Accumulators were another matter. His research into the causes of cancer gave rise to the suspicion that he was treating the disease, despite his denials. However, the investigations dragged on for years before the authorities took any action.

Meanwhile Reich was looking far beyond the fields of medicine and psychiatry. He was trying to establish that in orgone energy he had found an antidote to the nuclear bomb. He experimented with some radioactive material and the results were disastrous. Everyone involved went down with radiation sickness. It looked as though, like the Sorcerer's Apprentice, he had been playing with forces he could not control.

For the rest of his life he was dominated by the conviction that he had made a discovery which might save the world from a nuclear holocaust. Details of ORANUR (Orgonomic Anti-Nuclear Radiation) were published in the Bulletin and in a book issued in 1951. Only a physicist could assess them properly and I do not think any nuclear scientist agreed to do so.

After ORANUR we come to CORE (Cosmic Orgone Engineering). Reich devised an apparatus which he believed would make rain. This was publicly tested on 6th July 1953 at Hancock, Maine. The local blueberry growers had been badly hit by a prolonged drought and they were ready to try anything. Reich deployed his "cloud buster" and rain fell that evening, continuing for three days.

Whatever the truth about orgone, Reich's most loyal supporters must admit that the strain of persecution and what was practically ostracism from scientific circles clouded his judgment in the last phase. He sought what all philosophers have longed to find, a fundamental principle that would bring into a single, all-embracing system the varied phenomena of physics, biology and psychology. The world would not listen. His enemies hinted that he was showing symptoms of schizophrenia, or some said paranoia. One thing is clear, however wildly he might talk, the persecutions he had endured all his life were not all imaginary.

The American Medical Association and the American Psychiatric Association not only attacked him but made it difficult for psychiatrists trained in his methods to get suitable appointments. He was condemned also in such professional periodicals as the *Journal of the A.M.A.* and the *Bulletin of the Meninger Clinic*.

The Final Blow

The Food and Drug Administration struck in 1954. A court injunction was served restraining the distribution of Orgone Accumulators and the publication of the Orgone Institute Press. Reich refused to appeal in person and wrote a lengthy response denying the Government's right to interfere with scientific work. This was considered out of order and a decree was issued for the destruction of all accumulators. When the order was ignored a criminal contempt action was instituted.

This was a more serious matter and Reich was rash enough to refuse legal representation. The case wound its way through the tortuous procedures of the American courts: motions, appeals, amendments. Reich's position was not helped when he insisted on acting as Counsel for the Defence EPPO (Emotional Plague

Prevention Office). The final trial began on 3rd May 1956. Reich was arraigned with his co-worker Dr. Michael Silvert. On technical grounds there was no question that they were guilty. The charge on which they were tried was that they had defied a Decree of Injunction. Few expected that this would bring a prison sentence and Reich's friends were shocked when he was ordered to be imprisoned for two years, Michael Silvert for one year and one day, and the Wilhelm Reich Foundation was fined $10,000.

An appeal bought time but no alteration in the verdict. In March 1957 Reich entered the Danbury Penitentiary where he was diagnosed as a paranoid. He was then transferred to Lewisburg where there were psychiatric facilities. Reich, however, being paranoid, disdained treatment and the prison psychiatrists, not wishing, out of respect to the man, to put him through the ordeal of a second trial on the plea of legal insanity, pronounced him legally sane and competent. Nevertheless he was certainly a sick man. He died in prison of heart disease on 3rd November 1957.

Nothing can excuse the vindictiveness with which the F.D.A. agents tried to eradicate everything he had written as well as destroy the accumulator devices. The decree had merely ordered his hardcover books to be impounded, yet the entire stocks held at the Orgone Institute Press were seized and burned in a municipal incinerator. Fortunately copies of most of Reich's writings have been salvaged, though some of the papers and bulletins are either unobtainable or exceedingly rare.

It is convenient to divide the development of Reich's theories into three parts: (1) The theory of orgasm and the break with Freudian analysis; (2) The new technique of vegetotherapy; (3) Orgone therapy. The first two phases are widely considered as having given new and vital insights in psychiatry and have no necessary connection with the third phase. But, in all fairness and by any standards, Reich must be considered a brilliant man, and it would be outrageous if we judged him by his work during the later years of his life when he was mentally disturbed. Unfortunately, this is just what some of his critics appear to have done.

2 Psychoanalysis and Marxism

Today a psychoanalyst who was also an orthodox Communist would be a strange hybrid, if indeed one could be found. Fifty years ago, when Reich started his medical career and became a disciple of Freud, the combination already seemed odd, especially to Freud, but there was as yet no official opposition to analysis in the Soviet Union. In the years immediately after the Russian Revolution there was a period of such permissiveness that Reich thought that a new era of sexual freedom had begun. It proved to be a false dawn, but it could be argued that the reaction that followed was a betrayal of the hopes of the founders of Marxism.

The famous Communist Manifesto of 1848 predicted that the bourgeois family would vanish with the collapse of capitalism. Responsibility for the care and education of children would be taken over by Society.

If this seems merely rhetorical, Friedrich Engels, Marx's collaborator, made the point more plainly and in terms that fired Reich's imagination. He declared that monogamy had already broken down in practice, but this fact was concealed by the difficulty in getting a divorce. This one-sided hypocrisy would be swept away when capitalism was overthrown. A genuine sex-equality would then be possible for the first time: "But what new features will come into being? The answer will be given when a new generation has grown up; a generation of men who never in their lives chanced to buy a woman's surrender for money or any other social instrument of power; and a generation of women who have never happened to give themselves to a man for any consideration other than real love, nor refuse themselves to the man they love for fear of the economic consequences. When such people have come into existence, they will not care a brass farthing what people think today about how they should act; they will make their own practice for themselves, and their own public opinion, measured by this practice, as to the practice of each individual—and that will be the end of it." (*The Origin of the Family,* Chapter 2; translated in *A Handbook of Marxism,* Gollancz, 1936, p. 312.)

To Reich, these pronouncements could only mean that the economic revolution must not be separated from a sexual revolution. Marriage was bound up with the economic order and must stand or fall with it.

Inevitably he was accused of advocating "free love", just as Engels before him had been abused for supposedly upholding communal marriage. What they both urged was a greater sincerity in sexual relationships. The formality of a marriage ceremony was unimportant. Reich believed that under communism it would seem irrelevant. The commercialization of sex in marriage was a kind of prostitution. A woman need not marry for money in a crude sense, but she was still the helpless victim of a system which made marriage the price of economic security.

Harmful Family Ties

Since Reich wrote, the situation has improved and more and more women work outside the home. Nevertheless the problem is still with us. Marriage is no longer an insuperable obstacle to a career. Yet the changes have been more to the advantage of the middle-class professional woman than the working-class wife. If there are children, the problem is often insoluble. Nor is it only a question of money. Even women who can afford to employ home help or send their children to day nursery and later to a boarding-school often feel that to do so is to fail in their duty. They believe, and many psychoanalysts would agree, that the parents can provide a better background than the most luxurious institution. For Reich, on the other hand, the collectivization of society is incomplete unless it includes the care of the children. Family ties are part of the false ideology of marriage. They gloss over the sexual emptiness of the average marriage.

"One of the main difficulties", according to Reich, "was the inability of women—genitally crippled and unprepared for economic independence as they were—to give up the slave-like protection of the family and the substitute gratification which lay in their domination over the children."

He is referring here to the resistance in Russia, in the early period of the Revolution, to collectivization. A change of attitude to family life does not come about automatically as soon as the State takes over the economic machine. Old, deeply ingrained habits of mind persisted in Russia. They were based on infantile dependence. The material barriers to freedom might be removed but the emotional bonds remained.

Russian mothers were reluctant to give up the traditional control over the upbringing of their children. They belonged to a generation that had been conditioned to believe that family ties, including marriage itself, were sacred. If these ties dissolved the result would be anarchy, unless the authority of the parents was merely transferred to the State.

Reich certainly did not want one despotism to be exchanged for another. He was as much opposed to the authority of the State as to that of the family. He was against any sort of authoritarianism. The Soviet system was to develop into an extremely authoritarian regime, but though at first this did not seem inevitable, it was contrary to the original Marxist theory which Reich accepted.

Evolution of Monogamy

The theory was based on the investigations of a Victorian anthropologist, Lewis H. Morgan, on the evolution of social life. Morgan held that in its most primitive stage society was organized on the basis of some form of group marriage. The advent of the patriarchal type of family was related to the growth of private property as an institution. The husband was head of the family, and similarly the chief or king was head of the community. In both cases the patriarchal father-figure was vested with unquestioned authority.

Modern anthropologists do not accept Morgan's theory of universal stages in the passage of barbarism to civilization, but

21

this is an academic dispute which does not seriously affect Reich's main thesis. However authoritarianism may have arisen in the remote past, it seems bound up in the modern world with a repressive morality which extols monogamous marriage as an ideal.

Not only is marriage considered an essential condition for sexual intercourse, but all extra-marital relationships are forbidden. Children are brought up to prize chastity before marriage and to regard masturbation as wicked. When this strict moralism is enforced in a truly totalitarian regime the outward appearance is of neatness and order. In Mussolini's Italy divorce was not allowed and adultery (by the woman) was a crime, but as the admirers of Fascism pointed out, at least the trains ran on time. Reich's point is that this external orderliness conceals an inward disorder.

The emotional chaos behind the authoritarian façade is due to the fact that monogamy makes unnatural demands. It cannot be assumed that once a partner is chosen there will be no further sexual interest outside marriage in a lifetime. Furthermore, he felt that for a normal person such a restriction is impossible without repression, which is damaging. Usually it leads to the hypocrisy of a double standard.

The husband, conditioned in a society based on the sanctity of private property, looks upon his wife as a piece of property. If she is unfaithful to him, he declares that she has been "stolen" —as if anyone could really "steal" a woman, short of kidnapping one! But for the husband himself to commit adultery is not nearly such a serious matter. It is not only excused but even expected.

Today the situation is better in this respect than when Reich first attacked marriage. Divorce has become progressively easier and is now possible even in Italy. Yet the gain is not so great as some reformers suppose. Freedom is a mockery without economic security. That is why Reich regarded the social revolution and the sexual revolution as parts of the same fundamental process. Otherwise the majority of women will cling to marriage out of self-preservation.

Easier divorce is a palliative, not a solution to the marriage

22

problem. If legislation is all that is needed, the Russian experiment should have been an unqualified success. It was not.

Retreat from Freedom

In the confusion of civil war all traditional ideas were in the melting-pot. Sexual taboos seemed at first to belong to the Czarist ideology that had been overthrown. Divorce and abortion could be had practically for the asking. The only criterion for dissolving a marriage was that both partners wished to end it.

Two persons could live together, if they wished, without registering the fact, and no one thought the worse of them. If they registered their union (i.e. they married) and subsequently parted, alimony was only paid for six months, and not at all if either partner was fully employed. The traditional attitude to marriage as a lifelong foundation for rearing a family—"compulsive marriage", Reich termed it—disintegrated. The way forward seemed open to a totally new concept of sexual freedom on the lines Reich preached. Instead of taking that road the Soviet authorities took fright and retreated.

This was a bitter disappointment to Reich. He had pointed to Russia as an example of sexual emancipation. But in little more than a decade divorce and abortion were once more made difficult and a law punishing homosexuality was reintroduced. More significant than putting back the clock by legislation, since laws can always be changed again, was the revival of the older, reactionary attitudes to sex and marriage. For example, official propaganda began to praise family life and enjoin parents to exercise moral authority over their children. Weddings were once more made festive occasions and prizes were given for large families. *Pravda* stated that only a good family man could be a good Soviet citizen. "If anybody still contends that interest in the family is a petit-bourgeois characteristic, he belongs himself to the lowest category of petit-bourgeois."

When Reich visited Moscow in 1929 he was dismayed to find that the sex education given to young people was mainly about venereal disease and the dangers of causing pregnancy—obviously designed to frighten them from having intercourse. He asked the woman director of the Office for Maternal Health whether adolescents were being instructed in the necessity for and the use of contraceptives. She replied that such a measure would be incompatible with Communist discipline. Again, when Reich inquired at the Commissariat for Public Health how masturbation in adolescents was treated he was told "by diversion, of course". The suggestion that one should free a youngster of his guilt feelings was rejected by the doctor as "horrible".

What had become of the sexual revolution that had held out such promise? The economic and political revolution had followed Marxist theory, but neither Marx nor Engels provided any guidance on the sexual revolution apart from vague generalizations about the end of the bourgeois family. Their Russian followers were content to assume that once the economic structure of society was changed, human relationships would change of themselves. There was very little interest in the subject among the leaders of the Revolution. The voluminous writings of Marx, Engels and Lenin contain only a slight reference to sexual problems. All that Lenin had to say was given in an interview with Klara Zetkin criticizing the attitude of the younger generation. "Though I am not an ascetic it seems to me that this so-called 'new sexual life' of youth, and often also of older people, is often enough nothing but an expression of the good old bourgeois brothel," he said scathingly. He went on to condemn the theory that in a Communist society sexual gratification is as simple as drinking a glass of water. "Surely, thirst demands to be quenched. But will a normal individual, under normal circumstances, lie down in the gutter and drink from a puddle? Or even from a dirty glass?"

More in sorrow than anger Reich pointed to what was lacking in Lenin's statement. It did not say what young people should *do*. Lenin did not advocate abstinence as a solution to their problems, but his "glass of water" metaphor came to be used to deprecate sexual relations in adolescence. "Abstinence" became a slogan in universities on the grounds that the State could not afford to look after the children of students. It was as though no one had ever heard of contraception.

24

A New Morality

As a practising analyst Reich was convinced that what was missing from the Marxist model of society was any reference to the psychic structure of the individual. The instinctual drives with which we are born are given their direction by the type of society in which we develop. Thus a rigorous, puritanical society will create habits of obedience, conformism and sexual suppression. Morality will consist in rules and regulations imposed on the individual from outside.

Reich saw himself as the prophet of a new morality, a total transvaluation of existing values, based on self-regulation instead of compulsion. There could be no other meaning to freedom. To critics who said it was too dangerous to rely on the individual to regulate his own behaviour Reich replied that it was only dangerous when the psychic structure had been deformed by authoritarian morality. A man who is sexually satisfied has no desire to commit rape.

At the core of this new morality is Reich's conviction that sexual happiness is the most important thing in life. This essentially simple goal has nevertheless been evaded for thousands of years. It has been denied in the name of religion. Sex has been loaded with guilt and shame. Education has been used to drive natural instincts underground as soon as they appear at puberty.

If a new psychic structure is to be created we must begin with the child. The idea that parents should tolerate the genital play of children shocked Reich's contemporaries when he proclaimed it in sexual hygiene groups. The prospect does not seem so startling today, though the prosecution of *Oz* and *The Little Red Schoolbook* in 1971 shows that public opinion still has a long way to go.

Suppression of sex, Reich taught, not only results in a certain type of character—authoritarian in varying degrees—but leaves its imprint on the body. The musculature is so affected that full sexual satisfaction is impossible to attain, hence the desperate search for substitutes. The restless itch for novelty would not be felt, according to Reich, if we had a happy sex life. (This point will be dealt with in later chapters in more detail.)

25

Reich coined the terms Sexual-Politics and Sex-Economy to name a journal and institute which he founded to expound his views on a new morality and the formation of free, self-regulating individuals. He rejected the theory that economic needs were the mainstring of social development, as the Marxists taught. And so he found himself growing more and more out of step with both Marxism and official psychoanalysis.

Breach with Freud

It is ironical that at a time when Reich deviated from the Russian version of Marxism he should also have become an embarrassment to the International Psychoanalytical Association because of his connection with Communism. Whether this was the only reason for his expulsion from that body is obscure. Psychoanalysis was still taking shape and within certain limits differences of opinion could be tolerated.

Freud was not unduly perturbed by Reich's view that mental health depends on the capacity to experience orgasm. He seems to have regarded it, for a time at least, as a harmless eccentricity and Reich continued to train analysts at the Vienna Polyclinic until 1930. But his relationships with Freud were uneasy and he was deeply upset when Freud refused to accept him for a personal analysis.

On a somewhat theoretical level Reich was out of sympathy with Freud's decidedly pessimistic thesis in *Civilization and its Discontents*. Freud believed that the development of culture depended on instinctual renunciation. Culture, and all that is finest in civilization, was the fruit of sublimating, instead of gratifying, the instincts. Reich was totally opposed to any such renunciation. To have admitted that sexual repression was the price to be paid for human progress would make nonsense of his war on "sexual misery" and gospel of "sex-affirmation".

A more practical cause of disagreement lay in the radical views Reich was developing on treatment of patients. His general approach, of course, was very different from the ethical neutrality recommended by Freud. Reich had a new morality to preach.

26

He believed that this was part of a sexual revolution that would one day spread through society. Since so few people enjoyed their maximum possible potency, neuroses of one kind or another abounded.

According to Freud there are two groups of neuroses : one has a physiological origin, the other a psychological cause which could be traced to early experiences. Sexual deprivation, for example, may give rise to neurotic symptoms which clear up when a normal sexual life is resumed. But psycho-neuroses are more complicated and are usually treated by endeavouring to bring repressed material in the unconscious into full consciousness. It is as though a foreign body is lodged in an otherwise healthy organism and must be eliminated.

Reich questioned the value of "symptom analysis" as this was called. The symptoms which led neurotics to seek treatment might disappear, he argued, without removing the underlying character disturbance. So he was led by his own clinical experience to deny the existence of two distinct kinds of neurosis. He concluded that all neuroses had a double aspect, physiological and psychological. This is entirely in harmony with the psycho-somatic approach that is generally accepted today.

But he went further. Different symptoms there might be, but the root of the trouble was always the same. No neurotic, he claimed, is capable of experiencing a full and normal orgasm. There is only one thing wrong with neurotic patients, the lack of a full and repeated sexual satisfaction.

This remarkable simplification is one of Reich's most fruitful insights. Just as the rejection of psychological dualism cuts away a mass of redundant ideas and leaves one basic concept—the mind-body instead of mind *and* body—so the cumbersome jargon about neuroses is jettisoned. We are left with one simple yet fundamental idea and you do not have to be a psychoanalyst to grasp it. The idea, better to call it message, is that most people lack sexual fulfilment, and that this is an even more potent cause of misery than lack of material goods.

27

The Fear of Pleasure

Reich questioned how a "life-affirming" attitude could be created in a world that for thousands of years has submitted to an opposite, life-denying ideal? Or in plain language, how can the mass of people be enabled to pass from sex negation to sex affirmation? They have been so indoctrinated that they usually resist such a drastic change. They are *afraid* to be free.

We must admit that the anxiety aroused by pleasure, and above all by sexual pleasure, is a kind of sickness. Since it is natural to seek pleasure and avoid pain we cannot have been born with this strange anxiety. Individual therapy, even if it were always successful in removing anxiety, is available to few. The problem is therefore mainly social and must be attacked on that level.

Liberal reforms in a capitalist society, said Reich, only scratch the surface. But if there has been a social revolution there is an opportunity to change the individual character structure by a drastic reorganization of the educational system. Since parents and teachers are often sexually sick there must be centres where they can be re-educated, institutes for research on the physiology of sex and modes of contraception. Perhaps he went too far in suggesting that strong measures should be taken against teachers or parents found to be placing any kind of hindrance to infantile and adolescent sexuality. Facilities should be provided for adolescents to enjoy their new awareness of sexuality without interference or censure—special rooms, for example.

Character Armour

Although Reich failed to reconcile Freud and Marx some of his insights at the time are increasingly recognized as significant contributions to psychoanalytic theory. His attempt to discover the physiological basis of neurosis was an anticipation of much of the research in this field which has only lately won acceptance. He found that muscular tensions blocked the spontaneous surrender necessary for the maximum sexual pleasure. This anxiety

28

was not just a mistaken attitude of mind which could be removed by psychological techniques. The body itself had to be re-educated.

The originality of Reich's theory is his contention that the distortion only occurs in an authoritarian type of society. A strict moral standard in the family is repeated in the code taught in the school and embodied in the laws imposed by the government.

This is a vast conspiracy to surround sex with prohibitions. From an early age this repressive attitude not only arouses mental anxiety and feelings of guilt but also acts like a physical brake on sexual enjoyment. Chronic muscular rigidities, together with certain character traits, act like a kind of armour to protect the individual from unpleasure, though at the same time making him less sensitive to pleasure. The particular forms such a defence mechanism takes are what is commonly meant by a person's character.

"Character armour", as we shall see, is one of Reich's key concepts. He regarded it as the natural but unfortunate consequence of a patriarchal family with its emphasis on the virtues of obedience and submission. The task of the psychiatrist is to strip away the layers of "armour" which are an obstacle to mental health.

The first fundamental clash with psychoanalysis was caused by Reich's innovation in therapy by treating the musculature and posture direct instead of using free association and dream interpretation. In the earlier terminology, which he rejected, he approached the mind through the body instead of the body through the mind.

Reich had learnt from Marxist philosophy to be wary of treating the individual as a machine instead of an organism. The disturbance of any part cannot be completely localized, as would be the case if human beings were made like clockwork. Thus orgasm is not solely confined to the genitals. Its effects spread through the entire body—and so does its inhibition.

This conception can be represented pictorially by concentric circles. The individual mind-body (or psychic structure) is the smallest circle; it is enclosed by another circle, representing the family unit; and both are enclosed by another still larger circle, society. Whatever happens in any of these circles sends out repercussions to the whole. Thus, man is essentially a social animal; he is also very much at the mercy of the kind of society in which he is born.

Because of this web of interrelatedness, a social revolution is incomplete without a sexual revolution. Unless the two are seen as complementary, the social revolution will revert to authoritarianism and sexual suppression. That this happened in Russia seemed to Reich a sad confirmation of this theory.

3 The Emotional Plague

In the last, unhappy years of Reich's life his reaction to opposition was so violent that it became grotesque. He was a sick man who claimed that he alone knew the meaning of health, and that not only his enemies but the whole of society was infected by a psychic illness caused by a conflict between the longing for freedom and the actual fear of freedom. This he termed "the emotional plague" which he seriously argued in his early writings and we must not be misled by the extravagant outbursts during his trial in America when he described himself to the bewildered court as "Counsel for the Defence, Emotional Plague Prevention Officer".

He had used the term "psychic plague" in his penetrating analysis of Fascism. He understood the significance of Hitler long before it became apparent in England and America. After all, it forced him to leave Austria and Germany where his campaign for sexual reform was virulently suppressed. The obscene racialism of Streicher seemed to confirm Reich's view that the malaise had a sexual origin.

Many alternative explanations have been offered of the rise of Fascism, and obviously there can be no one explanation. It has been blamed on the economic plight of Germany before Hitler; on a conspiracy of powerful industrialists to subsidize a movement that would serve their interests; on biological aggression; and even on Original Sin. Reich's theory that it was the outcome of a widespread neurosis due primarily to sexual repression is also an over-simplification. But in fairness to Reich his views are more subtle and complex than they appear at first sight.

By sexual freedom he does not mean the promiscuity of a Casanova. It is rather freedom from the fears that were implanted in childhood and persist, largely unconsciously, thus robbing sexual behaviour of the spontaneity which brings the maximum satisfaction. This is not to deny that sex is enjoyable when it falls short of perfection. The really fundamental question that Reich sought to answer is why such a biological instinct as sex should become so inhibited? What purpose do the taboos and prohibitions serve?

Some light on this problem would be shed if we could find a society which had an entirely natural, unimpeded approach to sex. Reich believed that a community which fulfilled this requirement had been studied by his friend Malinowski in Melanasia.

Sex without Guilt

The Trobriand Islanders when Malinowski lived with them had very little sexual repression or sexual secrecy. The only sexual taboo was brother and sister incest. Apart from that their sexual development from early childhood was completely unhindered. They were allowed to indulge in any sexual activities appropriate to their age, and at puberty full intercourse was not merely tolerated but given every encouragement.

Here, then, is a society which gives social approval to pre-marital intercourse. Each village has a special dormitory set aside for the use of young lovers. There is nothing sordid or clandestine about these liaisons. By night they take place without the slightest sense of guilt, and by day small parties set out on love picnics. The affairs of the Islanders are characterized by a far greater refinement of taste than is often found in our present-day society.

It might be thought that sexual freedom in adolescence must make it difficult to settle down later to marriage. The contrary is the case. The Trobrianders do not experience the restless itch for novelty which, in the West, is often a sign of failure to obtain adequate satisfaction. On the whole their adult unions are happy and stable. If, however, a marriage breaks down it can easily be dissolved. Reich contrasts this attitude with "compulsive marriage" in a patriarchal society.

He writes: "The society the Trobrianders knew in the third

decade of our century, no sexual perversions, no functional neuroses, no psycho-neuroses, no sex murder; they have no word for theft; homosexuality and masturbation to them mean nothing but an unnatural and imperfect means of sexual gratification, a sign of disturbed capacity to reach normal satisfaction. To the children of the Trobrianders, the strict obsessional training for excremental control which undermines the civilization of the white race is unknown. The Trobrianders therefore are spontaneously clean, orderly, social without compulsion, intelligent and industrious. The socially accepted form of sexual life is spontaneous monogamy without compulsion . . ." (*The Function of the Orgasm* by Wilhelm Reich, Panther Books, 1968, p. 229.)

This arcadian existence has long been disturbed by the blessings of civilization and the attentions of missionaries. It may never have been quite so idyllic as Reich imagined. Although the Trobrianders felt no shame about sex they had a sense of decorum. Like almost all primitive peoples they had certain rules about clothing. "Modesty in the Trobriands", writes Malinowski, "requires only that the genitals and a small part of the adjacent areas should be covered, but the native has absolutely the same moral and psychological attitude towards any infringement of these demands as we have. It is bad and shameful and ludicrous in a degrading sense not to conceal, carefully and properly, those parts of the human body which should be covered by dress." (*The Sexual Life of Savages* by Bronislaw Malinowski, Routledge, 1929, p. 450.)

Challenge to Freud

One of the curious taboos was on the sexes eating together. Thus it was all right for a boy to take a girl into the bush for sexual intercourse, but people would be shocked if he asked her to lunch. Much more important for the psychoanalyst is the fact that the Oedipus conflict, as postulated by Freud, does not appear to occur in this matrilineal society. The role of the father is to play the part of a friend to his children, leaving their upbringing to his wife's brother.

Freud had assumed that from the age of two or three a boy

has an incestuous desire to possess his mother. This is not merely a resurgence of affection untouched by sexual feeling. He has begun to experience pleasurable feelings in his sex organs and learns to procure these by manual stimulation. He displays the organ of which he is proud to his mother. He wants to monopolize her attention and love, but the father stands in his way.

The child does not understand the real genital significance of his parents' relationship. He knows, however, that when the father is away he can more fully share his mother, and when the father returns this is not allowed. He feels an intense jealousy of his rival for the mother's love. But this longing for the mother and resentment of the father produces a conflict which is finally solved by repressing the situation.

Infantile masturbation is invariably punished either with some form of reprimand by the adored mother or, what is worse, by threats to cut off the organ with which he has been innocently playing. The fear of castration becomes all the more intense if the bewildered boy catches a glimpse of his sister's naked body. She seems to him to have undergone the dreadful punishment.

When the storms of the Oedipal conflict subside, most children enter a new stage of development, the so-called Latent Period. The emotional impulses that made such powerful demands are preserved in the unconscious, where they remain until puberty. Then they flare up in a confusion of fixations and inhibitions.

Freud held that the sequence of events was universal. His theory could not be *proved*, for practical reasons, but it could be *disproved* by producing a single case to the contrary. The Oedipal conflict might be widespread but evidently it did not exist among the Trobrianders. It might be argued that all Malinowski showed was that jealousy of the father could be replaced by jealousy of the uncle in a peculiar deviation of usual relationships. But this will hardly do because Freud emphasized the sexual nature of the boy's feelings. The uncle does not go to bed with the mother and arouse sexual jealousy.

The importance of this discrepancy for Reich was that it showed that the Oedipus situation, while it undoubtedly existed, was the result of culture, which can be different from place to place, not of biological constitution, which must be the same for all men. He clashed with Freud's biographer, Ernest Jones, who protested that the Oedipus complex, as found in Europe, was the "*fons et origo* of all culture".

Reich drew the opposite conclusion, namely, that sexual repression in infancy is not an unalterable part of our human nature but the result of sociological conditioning.

In one small part of the world there existed a society virtually free of sexual repression. The beneficial results could be plainly seen. Since children were not slapped down for playing with their genitals and were not made to feel guilty either about their sexual interests or their attitude to their parents, their development was smooth and uninterrupted. They did not go through a period between the age of five and puberty which was utterly devoid of sexual feeling. What Freud had called the Latent Period must be the result of repression, since it was entirely absent in a culture that was mainly permissive.

Erotic play in the years before puberty was followed by an equally innocent acceptance of sex as soon as intercourse became physically possible. The idea that sexual pleasure might be sinful would have been incomprehensible to the Trobrianders. They took it for granted that the purpose of living was to find happiness and that this meant satisfying the great basic drives of hunger and love.

Emotional Cripples

Is it possible to adapt the experience of primitive peoples in the South Pacific to the circumstances of the modern industrial world? Reich believed it was not only possible but essential if Western civilization was to be cured of its sickness. First we must get our priorities right. The quality of life mattered more than material goods and technological achievements. The great obstacle to fulfilment, he declared, was the neurotic character imposed on our children by the age of five. This stultified their emotional development. They grew up as emotional cripples and thwarted Nature took an appalling revenge, as the upsurge of cruelty under Fascism demonstrated.

Reich compared this sickness to a pestilence. His experience in running sex hygiene clinics seemed to confirm what he had learned from anthropology about infantile and adolescent sexuality. A number of primitive societies not far geographically from the Trobriand Islands were sternly disciplinarian, warlike and in some ways almost puritanical. Margaret Mead has described the Manus of the Admiralty Islanders as "Puritan to the core, committed to effort and work, disallowing love and the pleasures of the senses, they take quickly to the ways of the Western world, to money". Another people, the Mundugumor, have a form of social organization in which every man's hand is against every other man. "The women are as assertive and vigorous as the men; they detest bearing and rearing children and provide most of the food, leaving the men free to plot and fight." (*Male and Female* by Margaret Mead, Gollancz, 1950, p. 53.)

These and similar studies leave no doubt that character is more the product of social environment than heredity. Societies which are based on authority upheld by force, and which extol the Spartan values of discipline and endurance, prefer war to love. They illustrate Hobbes' famous description of life when it is unprotected by civilization as "nasty, brutish and short". Yet there are other societies, no less primitive, in which the members are co-operative, relaxed and unaggressive. To infer, as Reich did, that the greatest determining factor is the ability to have full sexual satisfaction was to go far beyond the evidence available to him, but undoubtedly it is one important factor.

He believed at the time that his theory, that freedom from neuroses depended on the capacity to achieve orgasm in the sense he defined it, was well within the Freudian framework. Even as late as 1945, in a preface to *Character Analysis*, he wrote: "Sex-economy has never taken a stand against the basic scientific findings of Freud . . . It is no more a rival of psychoanalysis than, say, Newton's law of gravitation is a rival of Kepler's law of harmony." But by then Reich had in fact moved as far away from Freud as from Marx.

Culture and Repression

(1) Freud held that the Oedipus conflict is common to all human beings, an inescapable phase of development. Reich denied that it was universal. It was the result of Nurture, not Nature. The seeds of neuroses were implanted by moralistic parents in early childhood, only to be exacerbated by the restrictions imposed at puberty, and still later by the straitjacket of monogamous marriage.

(2) Freudian psychoanalysts in the 1920's practised what came to be known as "symptom analysis". Neurotic symptoms were regarded as the expressions of a repressed infantile drive that has reappeared is a disguised form. The experiences which had caused the neuroses were brought to light by the methods of free association and dream interpretation.

Reich objected to this "atomistic" approach, as he termed the isolation of a particular symptom from the totality of psychic behaviour. The latter could still be disturbed even when the symptom being treated had apparently disappeared. "There are no neurotic symptoms", he wrote, "without a disturbance of the total character. Neurotic symptoms are, as it were, nothing but peaks of a mountain chain representing the neurotic character." (*The Function of the Orgasm*, p. 16.)

(3) Freud came to believe that repression, although regrettable, was necessary to the progress of civilization. He comes near to acknowledging Reich's claim when he admits "we cannot escape the conclusion that neuroses could be avoided if the child were allowed free play, as happens among many primitive races". But he goes on: "On the other hand we begin to perceive that such an early attempt at damming up the sexual instinct, such a decided partiality of the young ego for the external as opposed to the internal world, arising from the prohibition of infantile sexuality, cannot be without its effect upon the individual's later readiness for cultural growth. The instinctual demands, being forced from direct satisfaction, are compelled to take new directions which lead to substitutive satisfaction, and in the course of these detours they may become desexualized and their connection with their original instinctual aims may become looser.

37

And at this point we can anticipate the idea that much of our most highly valued cultural heritage has been acquired at the cost of sexuality and by the restriction of sexual motive force." (*An Outline of Psycho-Analysis* by Sigmund Freud, Hogarth Press, 1949, p. 72.)

To Reich, of course, any suggestion that sexual repression was other than harmful was anathema. The child who was subjected to severe toilet training and forbidden to masturbate was being made into a neurotic personality. This was the point of infection by "the emotional plague". As for Freud's idea that civilization is based on instinctual reunification, Reich could only accept it if by "civilization" was meant an authoritarian society—the very structure he wanted to overthrow.

The Death Instinct

Underlying Freud's basic outlook is a profound pessimism, a sense of the tragic element in life. He regarded the individual from the very beginning to be governed by a search for pleasureable sensations. But it is a fool's errand, an impossible quest. One might say that the intention that men should be happy is not included in the scheme of creation. What is called happiness in its narrowest sense comes from the gratification—most often instantaneous—of highly pent-up needs, and by its very nature can only be a transitory experience.

Reich, by contrast, is fundamentally optimistic in his philosophy. He denied that happiness was a goal forever out of reach. It was not some intrinsic flaw in the nature of life that doomed mankind, like Sisyphus, to eternal frustration. The fault lay in the social system, not in the nature of things. It was within man's power to re-fashion the system.

Needless to say, Reich also rejected Freud's concept of a Death Instinct. This is partly derived from the hypothesis that the nervous system has the function of abolishing stimuli. If you want to have sex you have it in order to stop wanting to have it. The nervous system is run on the principle of anything for a quiet life. But the only complete success in abolishing stimuli is to die. The compulsion to repeat earlier experiences, whether remembered or not, impels the organism to restore, not merely the absence of specific desire, but the earliest state of all—non-existence, death. The human being is therefore the battleground of two rival forces, one making for life and love (*Eros*), the other for death (*Thanatos*).

Few psychoanalysts followed Freud in what seemed a meta-physical speculation with abhorrent practical consequences. (For example, in *The Future of an Illusion* death is seen as the ultimate purpose of life and war as "inevitable and indeed biologically useful".)

Against Freud's binary forces Reich set a somewhat different pair of opposites: Life-affirmation and Life-negation. He preached this gospel throughout his stormy life whenever, as he saw it, "the emotional plague" threatened to destroy him.

Towards Mental Health

Reich was no mere dreamer, wild though some of his flights of fancy may now seem. He had no illusion that a handful of psychoanalysts could restore millions of men and women to mental well-being. He believed, however, that the winds of change were already blowing in the direction of a more rational attitude to sex. Writing in 1936 he remarked that a score of years earlier it would have been a disgrace for an unmarried girl not to be a virgin, but now the contrary was almost the case. Pre-marital intercourse no longer seemed so shocking.

"A few years ago, the idea that a girl of fifteen or sixteen—though she be sexually mature—had a boy-friend seemed absurd; today it has already become a matter for serious discussion; in a few more years it will be as much a matter of course as is today the right of an unmarried woman to have a sexual partner. A hundred years from now, such demands as that women teachers should have no sex life will provoke the same incredulous smile as does today mention of the times when men put chastity belts on their women." (*The Sexual Revolution*, p. 27.)

We have not had to wait a hundred years. Reich's attitude to the role of women antedated the Women's Liberation movement by forty years. He wrote in protest against the economic dependence of the woman on the man : "For, she is not only the sexual object of the man and the provider of children for the state, but her unpaid work in the household indirectly increases the profit of the employer. For the man can work at the usual low wages only on condition that in the home so much work is done without pay . . . If the wife is also employed she has to work overtime, without pay, if she wants to keep the home in order; if she does not do that, the household disintegrates more or less, and the marriage ceases to be a conventional marriage. In addition to these economic difficulties there is the fact that the woman, as a result of conventional sex education, is adapted not only to marital sex life, with all its sexual misery, compulsion and emptiness, but also with its external value and its settled routine which saves the average woman the necessity of thinking about her sexuality, and the struggles of an extra-marital life." (*Ibid.*, p. 146.)

What, then, did Reich propose? He had no faith in sex manuals which professed to improve marriages by new sexual techniques. They might help some individuals but they did not touch the real problem which was the institution of marriage itself. Again, divorce reform was necessary because of the intolerable strains of an indissoluble union. But no amount of tinkering with the institution of marriage could provide a final solution.

It might be objected that whether or not a wedding ceremony is retained, a lasting sexual relationship is only different in name from marriage. Reich does not wholly avoid this contradiction. He is at pains to show that a permanent sexual relationship is preferable to a temporary relationship because it makes the quest for a suitable partner unnecessary and thus liberates time and energy for other achievements. Yet he holds that none of the conditions which are necessary to the success of a lasting relationship can be realized, except by a few individuals, in an authoritarian society.

So we are back at square one. The social order and sexual relationships are so interrelated that it is impossible to change one without changing both. Whilst still under the influence of Marxism, Reich was sceptical of the value of reforms that fell short of revolution; nevertheless, he advocated a radical programme of reform, *faute de mieux.*

The real problem was how to be rational about sex—or anything else— in an irrational society. Practically everyone has been contaminated by the environment. That is why there is an element of truth in the objection that to upset conventional moral codes abruptly must result in social chaos. Reich had to admit that too sudden a dose of freedom would go to people's heads. The process of liberation must inevitably be gradual.

Education in Freedom

Reich believed that the best hope of the future lay in a more rational education of succeeding generations, a view with which it would be difficult to disagree. From their earliest years children should be accustomed to the sight of nudity, and they should be told as much as they can understand of what sex is all about. If they wish to watch sexual intercourse Reich saw no good reason why this should be refused, an idea which outraged many at the time and is still totally unacceptable to many. But why should parents wrap up information about sex in elliptical and woolly language? Why should they not have the courage to say that sexual intercourse is pleasurable to grown-ups just as playing with the genitals is pleasurable to the child?

Intercourse can begin at adolescence, provided there is instruction about birth control, and Reich's experience with young people in his work in hygiene clinics convinced him that abstinence at this period—say, between the age of fifteen and eighteen—was positively harmful. It is very seldom complete since most young people practise masturbation, and this he regarded as decidedly inferior. It arouses a more intense guilt feeling than intercourse because it is often burdened with incest fantasies, whereas intercourse makes such fantasies superfluous.

On the other hand, Reich is careful to stress that it would be irresponsible to encourage adolescents to follow their impulses *before* they have received adequate education. It is not only necessary to explain the use of contraceptives but to ensure that they are readily available. And Reich did not realize what has

41

since become apparent: that many of the teenage girls who become pregnant simply did not bother to take precautions. They are the victims of their own fecklessness, not ignorance. In view of this it may be unwise, after all, to emphasize the drawbacks of masturbation as a substitute to intercourse.

Reich makes a distinction between "compulsive morality" and "natural morality". By the former he means a set of regulations imposed from outside by the State or Church. Their object is to curb the sexual impulse by instilling a fear of sex in children, discouraging sex at puberty, and confining it for adults in the bonds of marriage. Compulsive morality is essentially "sex-negating", but natural morality is "sex-affirming".

Natural morality implies that human nature in itself is good; and all that is bad in human behaviour is due to the distorting effect of environment. Morality, therefore, should not be a matter of rules but the natural response of a healthy individual to the situations of life. He will not have to look up an answer book to find out what's right or wrong. He will have no impulses that require excessive inhibiting.

This fortunate state is brought about by the attainment of "orgastic potency", the full meaning of which we shall consider in the next chapter. Briefly, it is the capacity to completely surrender, joyously and spontaneously, at the moment of sexual climax. This lost Eden cannot be fully recovered by the majority of people until society is cleansed of the "emotional plague". So far from the collapse of traditional morality being a sign of decadence, it removes the main obstacles to mental health.

Although Reich began as a Marxist he owes much more to Rousseau, a still earlier pioneer of progressive education, who taught that to be good is to live in accordance with the potentialities of one's nature. For Reich this meant, first and foremost, the uninhibited enjoyment of sex. To those critics who protested that liberty would end as licence he replied that the evils they feared only arose when sex was obstructed.

"The healthy individual has no compulsive morality because he has no impulses which call for moral inhibition. What anti-social impulses may be left are easily controlled, provided the basic genital needs are satisfied. All this is shown clearly in the practical behaviour of the individual who has become orgastically potent." (*The Sexual Revolution*, p. 6.)

The trouble is that the behaviour of individuals who are "orgastically potent" has not been shown clearly by Reich because there are so few of them. Sweeping generalizations based on intuition rather than evidence were common among the early disciples of Freud and nothing has done more to bring psychoanalysis into disrepute.

It now remains to examine in more detail what Reich meant by the key concepts of "genital character" and "orgastic potency".

4 The Theory of Orgasm

One of Reich's most original and debatable claims is that every neurosis is symptomatic of sexual failure. To express this more accurately, neurosis is not merely the result of sexual disturbance in the broad sense employed by Freud, but of a disturbance in a narrower, more precise sense. So it is no criticism of Reich to point to people who do not seem to be sexually inadequate and yet are nevertheless neurotic. Reich is using a different terminology.

The key concept is orgasm. By this he means a joyous, spontaneous surrender in which the whole body, especially the pelvis, is involved in involuntary movements of varying degrees. It cannot be measured entirely by subjective feelings, since many enjoy sexual intercourse without achieving what Reich calls "orgastic potency".

He makes a distinction between sexuality in a general sense, which may take differing forms, and genital satisfaction, which is exactly what the words suggest. He writes: "Up until 1923, the year when the orgasm theory was born, sexology and psychoanalysis knew only of ejaculative and erective potency . . . [These] are nothing but indispensable pre-requisites for orgastic potency. Orgastic potency is the capacity for surrender to the flow of biological energy without any inhibition, the capacity for complete discharge of all dammed-up sexual excitation through involuntary pleasurable contractions of the body. Not a single neurotic individual possesses orgastic potency; the corrolary of this is the fact that the vast majority of humans suffer from a character neurosis." (*The Function of the Orgasm*, p. 114.)

Transformation of Character

The sweeping statement that nearly everyone is in some degree neurotic, and that this is due to undischarged sexual energy, is based on his own clinical experience. Freud was increasingly sceptical of this approach, since the treatment Reich developed deviated sharply from psychoanalytical practice at that time. For example, it was a rule that the analyst should not be seen, that he should be ethically neutral, a kind of screen on which the patient could project his transferences.

Reich, on the other hand, went all out to free his patients of their genital inhibitions by any means that worked. None of his patients was pronounced cured unless he (or she) was at least able to masturbate without guilt feelings. As for the curious rule imposed by many analysts that while under treatment a patient must observe sexual abstinence, Reich dismissed it with scorn.

The aim of this kind of therapy was avowedly to dissolve an emotional blockage which prevented full genital surrender. As this began to be removed the character of the patient was expected to change. Previously he might have had strict moral views, for example, on pre-marital chastity or adultery. Quite spontaneously, Reich claimed, the prohibitions and conventions of society—at least those referring to sex—looked alien and queer. Sometimes the establishment of a "genital character" led to a revolt against routine work. Concomitantly there might be a growth of tolerance and social conscience.

Those women patients who had previously carried out their "conjugal duties" in a loveless marriage found they could no longer submit to their husbands' demands. Something now had come to life in them, a self-awareness, a sense of liberation. Furthermore, a woman who had been released from crippling inhibitions and who experienced complete genital fulfilment could no longer be content with less. She broke away from conventional morality if there was no other means of gratifying her need for love.

Reich is at pains to show that the "genital character" does not turn to loveless promiscuity. On the contrary, a patient who formerly had a restless itch constantly to change partners might become perfectly satisfied with just one partner.

Monogamy of a purely legalistic kind is another matter. Reich called this "compulsive morality" and regarded it as part of the fetters which tradition fastened on the individual. It renders its

45

victims submissive by inculcating the idea that marriage is indissoluble. In Reich's view an intimate relationship ought to last as long as it gives satisfaction, and that can be a very long time for the orgastically potent.

Forty years ago such a doctrine sounded much more shocking than it seems today. It was inevitable that Reich should be accused of preaching free love and using quite impermissible methods in analysis. Both these charges are based on a misunderstanding of what he really taught. His theory, rightly or wrongly, was that Casanova, who is only interested in fresh conquests, is a sexual failure. If he were capable of full sexual satisfaction he would not need to keep changing partners. The nymphomaniac, the fetishist, the sadist and the masochist were all suffering from a neurosis which could not be cured by attacking individual symptoms but only by going to the sexual roots of their sickness.

Freudian analysis, by contrast, was a piecemeal method and could take years, with a very uncertain result. Even if it were successful in bringing to light some forgotten incident in childhood which made a man a festishist or exhibitionist or impotent, the underlying neurotic condition might still remain and show itself in the formation of different symptoms. Instead of this "atomistic" approach Reich sought to treat the patient as a whole person, to restore him to mental health by breaking down his inhibitions. The proof of success was the ability to have orgasm in Reich's special, psychosomatic sense.

The Meaning of Orgasm

What did he understand by orgasm? For the most part the sexual act goes through well-known phases for both sexes in which tension builds up to a climax and is then released. The anatomical details have been minutely described by Masters and Johnson in their study, *Human Sexual Response.* They had access to data which Reich would have warmly welcomed because of its emphasis on bodily changes rather than psychology. But Reich's view is nonetheless distinctive.

The first phases he describes are much the same as we find in any marriage manual. They could hardly be different. He

46

approves any kind of foreplay that leads to intercourse, but does not approve of foreplay as an end in itself. This he considers to be a neurotic symptom. The man may have an erection or ejaculate, but that is not what Reich means by orgasm. So, too, the woman may experience vaginal contractions, but unless she is able to let herself go completely and blindly, it is not the Reich orgasm.

In phase two the pleasurable excitement increases and the man has a stronge desire for penetration whilst the woman longs to receive his erect penis. Because of this her vagina is moist and lubricated. The pleasurable sensation becomes more concentrated on the genitals than other parts of the body, which is not to to deny that love-play still plays a part.

A feature to which Reich attaches special importance is that although consciousness is narrowed to exploring all channels of sensation, it is not eclipsed as it should be at the moment of orgasm. The gradual progress towards the next, more intense phase is facilitated by slow, gentle movements. The man who cannot bear to wait and is overwhelmed by nervous haste is either afraid of premature ejaculation or is yielding to a sadistic urge to penetrate as deeply and violently as possible. His impatience, whatever the cause, seldom gives pleasure to his partner.

From Voluntary to Involuntary

There is no significant difference as yet in the activities of the man and woman. They both participate in complementary, rhythmic movements. At least, that is if they are to meet with success. Many women derive no enjoyment from intercourse. To some extent this may be due to faulty technique or memories of a disillusioning honeymoon. A deeper reason—and by no means always unconscious—is a fear of sex induced by guilt. Reich regards mere technique as of limited value since it does not touch the roots of the problem. If at this stage the partners have not begun to co-operate harmoniously and without an inhibiting self-consciousness, there is no likelihood that they will be roused to the point of mutual surrender.

If they wish their congress to last as long as possible, this is the time to slow down or even pause. Reich warns against talking or any form of distraction at any point during the sexual act as this keeps the mind too alert and on a superficial plane. But expressions of tenderness, on the other hand, induce the right state of mind.

The next phase has an altogether new quality. So far the situation has been under conscious control. If it remained voluntary there would be no hope of reaching the climax which, according to Reich, is essentially involuntary. Any interruption now would be fatal. The rhythm must be undisturbed and so gradually take on the character of an involuntary action.

The smooth swinging of the pelvis without conscious effort is one sign of "orgastic potency". It must occur without deliberately trying. Any conscious control of these movements destroys their reflex character.

As the slow, deep muscular contractions are intensified the excitement spreads to the whole body. Breathing becomes deeper, the heart beats faster, the walls of the vagina contract so that they grip the penis. At this moment the peak is nearly reached. The accumulated nervous tension is almost at bursting point, causing the body to sweat, the limbs to tremble and sometimes convulse in the semblance of mild epilepsy.

It is easy to mistake this for the final release, and if the man withdraws, he leaves his partner tense and restless. She has been climbing towards the peak only to be baulked when success seems within her reach. Even if he ejaculates before she is ready, he should on no account disengage himself. Indeed this is hardly possible if the sex act has been performed throughout with loving gentleness.

Orgasm is preceded by a kind of clouding of consciousness. Sensation is focused on the genitals clamouring for a discharge of pent-up sexual energy. Once it breaks through the dam, it floods the whole body. According to Reich: "The acme thus represents the point at which the excitation changes its direction. Up to the point of the acme the direction is towards the genital, and at the point of the acme it turns into the opposite direction, i.e. towards the whole body. The complete flowing back of the excitation towards the whole body is what constitutes gratification.

48

Gratification means two things: shift of the direction of flow of excitation in the body, and unburdening of the genital apparatus." (*The Function of the Orgasm*, p. 119.)

Objections to Reich's Theory

In what way, it may be asked, does Reich's concept of orgasm differ from that of other investigations in this field? The involvement of the whole body is not new, though its importance was not fully recognized by Freud. The futile controversy about the rival merits of clitoral and vaginal orgasm needlessly complicated the problem. We now know that no such distinction is valid.

Freud, and many psychoanalysts who followed him, believed that clitoral orgasm is an expression of immaturity, whereas vaginal orgasm is a sign of maturity. This conclusion was reached by *a priori* reasoning rather than observation. It is certainly quite false. Ruth and Edward Breches, describing the laboratory studies of Masters and Johnson, declared categorically: "There is neither a purely clitoral orgasm nor a purely vaginal orgasm. There is only one kind of orgasm from a physiological point of view—the sexual orgasm." (*An Analysis of Human Sexual Response*, André Deutsch, 1967, p. 84.)

This appears to support Reich's view that orgasm is a total reaction and cannot be split into two different types. On the other hand, the possibility that a completely satisfying climax can be achieved by artificial means would make the elaborate training of pelvic movement seem unnecessary. If Masters and Johnson are correct, auto-stimulation is actually more effective than intravaginal coition since it is more likely to induce multiple orgasms. They state: "From an anatomic point of view, there is absolutely no difference in the response of the pelvic viscera to effective sexual stimulation, regardless of whether the stimulation occurs as a result of clitoral area manipulation, natural or artificial coition, or, for that matter, from breast stimulation alone . . . The human female's physiological responses to effective sexual stimulation develop with consistency, regardless of the source of the psychic or physical stimulation." (*Western Journal of Surgery, Gynæcology and Obstetrics*, September–October 1962.)

If an electric vibrator is just as good as a human lover, the intense personal relationship which Reich regarded as the goal of the orgastically potent can be dispensed with. But Masters and Johnson do not, of course, say anything so absurd. They are speaking strictly from an anatomical point of view. And their observations were made on volunteers, not on people who, given a choice, preferred masturbation to intercourse.

Reich would say that to prefer masturbation, or some sexual deviation, is a sign of psychic malaise. Potency, on his definition, is much more rare than the ability to have an erection and ejaculate, and more for a woman than vaginal spasms. The essence of orgasm is the virtual loss of consciousness, the loss of control over bodily movements, the ecstatic surrender in release.

Reich is saying that unless this ultimate perfection can be obtained the individual is suffering from some degree of emotional blockage, and that this is indeed the fate of the majority of people. It is not enough to enjoy sex; we have to enjoy it in a special way.

I find this unconvincing. I have suggested that a distinction should be made in women between sexual satisfaction in general and orgasm in particular. "There are those married women whose sexual satisfaction consists essentially in giving pleasure to their husbands without achieving a sexual climax themselves; others rarely obtain sexual pleasure on the genital level at all." (*The Sexual, Marital and Family Relationships of the English Woman*, Hutchinsons, 1956, Eustace Chesser *et al.*)

I do not wish to minimize the influence of orgasm and sexual satisfaction on marital happiness. It is, however, quite possible for a woman to find sexual relationships extremely pleasurable without experiencing the extreme surrender which Reich holds up as an ideal. The danger of stressing such an ideal is that many people who were otherwise reasonably content with their love-life become dissatisfied. They begin to worry because perfection seems to elude them. The pleasure they once had in deep petting is made by Reich to look suspect and almost perverted. The same type of situation can, and often does, apply to men, although there are of course biological and cultural differences.

One reason why Reich looks askance at marriage manuals is

that the conscious pursuit of orgasm is not only contrary to his teaching, but strongly condemned by him. What we should aim at, he contends, is the conscious pursuit of psychic health, which is a different thing. The "genital character" has abolished the obstacles to orgastic potency. This is not to be regarded as some rare superhuman accomplishment deserving a gold medal in sex Olympics, but as the normal condition of a healthy human being. At some point civilization took a wrong turning and we have lost our original innocence. Our natural development is distorted by sexual taboos that create a sense of guilt.

Character Armour

Although Reich considered himself a Marxist, he is much nearer in this respect to Rousseau's concept of living in accordance with one's true nature. Man is born free, yet is everywhere in chains, said Rousseau. These chains are fastened on us by an authoritarian society to keep the majority of people satisfied with the *status quo*.

Reich speaks of "armour" instead of chains, but it comes to the same. Originally his concept of "character armour" was introduced in examining the problem of compulsion neurosis. Thus some individuals feel compelled to keep washing their hands, to eat or drink excessively, etc. According to Freud these symptoms always hide anxiety. In theory the anxiety can be released in the course of analysis; but in practice this does not always happen.

The individual has acquired certain habits of mind that protect him from becoming aware of his own repressed emotions. Habits and attitudes which have been developed to shield the individual from painful feelings constitute what Reich calls "character armour". In one way it is an evasion, a sweeping of dirt under the carpet. The price to pay is that whereas we are protected from disagreeable feelings our sensitivity is so dulled that we cannot feel as much pleasure as is possible, especially in sex.

"It is", writes Reich, "as if an affective personality put on an armour, a rigid shell on which the knocks from the outside world as well as the inner demands rebound. This armour makes the

51

individual less sensitive to unpleasure, but it also reduces his capacity for pleasure and achievement." (*Character Analysis*, p. 310.)

The concept was extended from the treatment of compulsion neurosis to the more general aim of therapy. That aim, in Reich's system, should be to transform the character of the individual. He must be stripped of the armour which protects him from the demands of his essential nature, above all from uninhibited sexual expression. The armour has allowed a pool of undischarged sexual energy to accumulate and it is this source of energy which nourishes neuroses, no matter how much they may differ from each other. The "unarmoured" individual has won complete inner freedom. He has become, in Reich's terminology, "a genital character". That is to say, he has been freed of all obstructions to "orgastic potency".

In another vivid metaphor Reich likens the character armour to the covering of a bladder. The sexual urge is like a force inside the bladder, directed outward and therefore causing it to expand. But if the bladder is of metal instead of elastic skin, it cannot expand. The only way to obtain relief from the increasing tension would be for the bladder to burst, i.e. to experience total discharge of sexual energy in orgasm. The rigidity of the armour makes this impossible.

The Roots of Anxiety

Again and again Reich uses the analogy of "bursting". If sexual energy approaches bursting point and cannot find an outlet, the whole psyche is disturbed. The inevitable result would be anxiety. For if the expansion which would normally be pleasurable only gives rise to painful sensations, because it is blocked, a fear of pleasurable excitation must develop. Various theories would then be invented about the sinfulness of pleasure. People with such ideas would band together and form a society or a religion dedicated to a puritanical ideal. Some would turn away from life altogether and seek the mystical peace of Nirvana. All these stratagems are attempts to escape from deep-seated anxiety.

The anxiety is as much a physical as a mental condition. A child, for example, frightened by fear of punishment, holds his breath and pulls in his abdomen. This is a natural reaction that anyone can test for himself. Posture and musculature can undoubtedly reflect mental states.

Reich recalls how he treated a man who strongly resisted bringing to consciousness his passive-homosexual fantasies. It was shown in his bodily condition by an extreme stiffness of neck. When his resistance was broken down the physical repercussions were somewhat alarming. The energy which had been bound by his stiff neck broke loose and for several days produced symptoms which worried Reich, though they seemed to confirm that he was on the right track. He concluded that muscular armour and character attitudes are inseparable.

The armoured character fails sexually, not just because of ideas or beliefs he may have about sex, but because his inbuilt anxiety makes it impossible for him to free himself. At the critical moment —or perhaps all the the time—his abdomen is drawn in, he is unable to allow his pelvis to swing in effortless rhythm. He is like someone driving a car with the hand-brake on.

Psychosomatic approach

As Reich developed this theory he moved still farther away from Freud. Orthodox psychoanalysis sought to remove anxiety by purely psychological means. Reich attacked the neurosis through the body itself. A patient might suppress or distort the truth in conversation, but it would be difficult to lie with his body. If he entered the room with his head hanging down, his back curved, his whole demeanour the reverse of confident and forceful, there would be no need to rely on his verbal account.

It was unheard of at that time for the analyst to touch his patient. Reich had no such qualms. He set to work to loosen the stiff neck and pelvic muscles and was rewarded often in a quite dramatic fashion.

Reich called his treatment vegetotherapy. It is based on a rejection of the dualistic theories of mind and body which so many psychologists hold tacitly even though they may deny it. The term "vegetative" used to be applied to what is now more usually called the autonomic system. The word was taken over by Reich in the early 1930's, the middle period before he turned away from psychiatry to what was regarded as the bizarre theory of orgone energy.

Many think that Reich's must valuable contribution was to provide a psychosomatic foundation for psychiatry. He went farther and showed that there was a vital connection between psychology and sociology. A great deal of what he said about the mechanism of orgasm has since been confirmed, albeit with some modification. But the claim that *all* neuroses are signs of sexual failure of one kind or another is not supported by evidence. It could be made plausible if we defined psychic health in such a way that ill-health can only be due to sexual malfunctioning, which is a tautology and tells us nothing.

Science progresses by discovering a unifying principle in the bewildering profusion of Nature. The success of this method in the physical sciences encourages psychologists to search for general laws governing human behaviour. The instinct of self-preservation could be one such principle, using the concept in a wide sense to include the restoration of equilibrium which has been disturbed. This led Freud to postulate a Death Instinct, but Reich would have none of it. Instead, Reich advanced a more optimistic, forward-looking philosophy which has a great deal in common with the anarchism of the New Left today.

If he had been content to emphasize the importance of sexual satisfaction, he would have been expressing in more technical terms the life-affirming gospel which D. H. Lawrence was preaching at the same time. But human nature is too complex to be embraced in a single formula. It has not been proved that there are no serious frustrations apart from sex. Reich's own life demonstrates to the contrary.

5 The Technique of Vegetotherapy

Reich was a materialist, and this profoundly affected his entire outlook. The central importance he attached to orgasm is materialistic in the sense that orgasm is a material fact and not just a state of mind. In psychoanalysis, for example, failure to reach orgasm, as in cases of sexual frigidity or impotence of one form or another, is attributed to mental attitudes. The patient is encouraged to dredge the unconscious and bring to the surface forgotten memories of some past traumatic experience. The patient's body hardly enters the discussion. The analyst's language contains such terms as "unconscious", "id", "ego", and "super-ego". There is no mention of "nerves", "muscles", "organs", "pelvis", etc.

Freud himself was a materialist in the sense that his early hope was to locate the physical basis of neuroses. It proved too difficult, and the model he constructed of the mind was more fruitful. He would not have denied that it had a bodily correlation, but as the analytical method developed this was little more than a theoretical acknowledgement. The only contact the analyst had with his patient was verbal.

There does not seem to be any intrinsic reason why analysis should not, with advantage, be accompanied by some kind of physical treatment. In its early days the theory was still being developed, and there were rebels against a rigidly orthodox line. Jung and Adler broke away completely, but Reich was actually training analysts and he did not at first see anything incompatible with his own insights into the fundamentals of Freudian teaching. Some of Reich's ideas at this stage might well have been incorporated in psychoanalysis with profit. It is quite possible that if Reich had not been excommunicated by the Freudian church, he would have been spared his future aberrations.

Body and Mind

The starting-point of the technique he called "vegetotherapy" is that our basic traits are impressed on the body. A confirmed pessimist not only has a gloomy outlook; his misery is written on his face, on the way he walks or slumps in a chair. This is a very simplified example, but there are countless more complex cases in which a skilled diagnostician can read the main trends of a person's character and any neurotic tendencies.

So far, there is nothing particularly new in the idea. A man applying for a job is often judged to some extent by the way he speaks, holds himself and walks. If he keeps his chin up, his shoulders back, and his voice is steady and unperturbed, it strongly suggests that he has self-confidence. Another man, who comes nervously into the room, keeps his thumbs tucked in clenched hands, speaks haltingly in a low voice, indicates just the opposite.

Reich's originality is to carry this well-known behaviour pattern much farther. He regards a person's general bearing and posture, not merely as a reflection of his state of mind, but as *part* of it. To employ the old terminology of body and mind, which he rejects, the state of the body is as likely to influence the state of the mind as vice versa.

Feelings of anxiety do not exist simply "in the head". Over a long period they affect the musculature. The way a man breathes may lead to permanent inhibitions, especially in regard to sex. Anxiety symptoms can obstruct the orgastic reflex.

This, again, is scarcely a discovery. Freud contended that anxiety is the central problem of neuroses. And anxiety is expressed in somatic terms by such muscular behaviour as flexor contraction and extensor inhibition. The bodily response to fear is to adopt the position that seems safest: immediately to become passive, "play possum", and as in falling to bend the knees and either bunch the arms or use them as a shield. When this type of reaction is repeated from childhood it becomes such a deeply ingrained habit that reversal is difficult if not impossible.

We are not born with these habits. They are a conditioned reflex induced by fears planted during the oedipal situation, i.e.

by the fourth year. In fact, there is no necessity for such fears, for a more rational upbringing would enable a child to develop without constraint. The parents are responsible but they are not necessarily to blame. They, too, have been conditioned. They brainwash the child just as they have been brainwashed by a society which is mainly concerned to maintain its structure intact.

This theme runs through all Reich's writings and shows how deeply he continued to be influenced by Dialectical Materialism long after he broke with the Communist Party. It is not original, any more than is the observation that conditioned reflexes have an anatomical aspect. Repeated anxiety often shows itself in a faulty posture, which is characteristic of many emotionally disturbed persons.

Maturity of Posture

If it is asked why one posture is more correct than another, the answer is simple. To keep erect we have to overcome the tendency of the body, which is naturally top-heavy, to fall down. A sculptured figure will not stand upright on two feet unless they are fixed to a pedestal. The problem is solved by a human being, unique among mammals, by a built-in mechanism to counteract gravity. When the result is achieved with the minimum of effort, we can speak of the posture as "correct" or "mature".

A Judo wrestler falls without hurting himself because he does not try to interfere with the instinctive response of his body. In other words, he does not flex his muscles because he has no fear of being hurt. Nor is a drunken man or a somnambulist afraid, neither of whom usually damages himself. If you watch a matador turning gracefully on his vertical axis to avoid a charging bull, it is obvious that he is turning with a minimum expenditure of effort. The same can be said of a ballet dancer and all who use their bodies in the way they have been designed. But have we any reason to suppose that wrestlers, matadors and ballet dancers are less neurotic than other members of the community? Do we know that they all enjoy orgastic potency? We do not know whether this is, or is not, the case.

There is no need to assert that there is only *one* way in which

57

emotional disturbances are reflected in bodily behaviour, but there is certainly an association which varies considerably from individual to individual. It is also true that if we wish to preserve a reflex, the less we think about it the better. Every golfer knows that as soon as he becomes conscious of how he should swing a club he is likely to make a bad shot.

More important is the fact that the orgasm reflex is partly or even wholly inhibited if the individual is anxious. But it is another matter to suppose, as Reich does, that release of sexual tension is incomplete unless the oscillations of the pelvis occur as he describes. The most that can be safely claimed is that muscular rigidity is liable to act as a brake.

One aspect of vegetotherapy did break new ground. Reich applied quite literally his belief that the patterns of muscular behaviour are "functionally identical" with character traits. Or, as he states it, muscular armour and character serve the same purpose of holding back a repressed emotion. The tension due to repression and the relaxation due to its removal are both somatic processes which can be observed.

The New Technique

How can the tension be relieved by physical means? The technique Reich devised dissolved the chronic muscular rigidity which had developed as a defence mechanism. He found it was possible to release anxiety by working at first on tensions around the eyes. The chronic stare of some patients was due, he thought, to chronic rigidity in the eyelids. Similar patterns may be found all over the body, especially around the mouth and chin, the abdomen and pelvis. By loosening and encouraging the movements of muscles around the mouth and chin suppressed feelings of anger and disgust can be released.

Facial expression may serve as a mask concealing suppressed aggression. A stiff upper lip can express a stoical attitude to sentiment although unconsciously there is a longing for affection. "Many people have a mask-like facial expression", Reich wrote. "The chin is pushed forward and looks broad; the neck below the chin is 'lifeless'. The lateral neck muscles which go to the

58

breast-bone stand out as thick cords; the muscles under the chin are tense. Such patients often suffer from nausea. Their voice is usually low, monotonous, thin. This attitude, too, one can reproduce in oneself. One has only to imagine that one is trying to suppress an impulse to cry; one will find that the muscles of the floor of the mouth become very tense, the muscles of the whole head become tense, the chin is pushed forward and the mouth becomes small. In this condition one will try in vain to talk with a loud, resonant voice." (*The Function of the Orgasm.*)

There is ample testimony that Reich was often successful in this combination of analysis and physical manipulations. A. S. Neill, the educationalist, and Nic Waal, a Norwegian psychiatrist, pay grateful tributes to the treatment they received. Both admit it was drastic and sometimes painful. How far this was due to the impact of Reich's powerful personality is an open question. He might have gained some measure of success with a different kind of therapy. Yet the path he opened up has so many advantages over the purely Freudian method that it needs to be explored on a far wider scale. There must be many who wish that Reich had been content to do so.

The physical contact with the analyst was neither massage nor masturbation. The enormous influence of "touching" was not appreciated in Reich's day. Lately "Encounter Groups" and "touch-ins" have turned serious as well as popular attention to this subject. To understand how the method was used, let us look at a case history.

Reich at Work

A technician of twenty-seven years of age consulted Reich because of excessive drinking. He was unhappily married and not able to establish a relationship with another woman. He could no longer take any interest in his work. He was quite unable to show any aggression. Socially he felt obliged to be affable and polite to the point of agreeing with opinions he did not hold.

The first thing for the analyst to notice is the outward signs of "character armour". This patient walked clumsily with a forced stride. His posture suggested submissiveness. His facial expression and eyes were curiously blank. The mouth was small and tight and hardly moved when speaking.

Reich decided to start with the facial expression. He kept drawing attention to the rigidity of the mouth until an involuntary tremor of the lips resulted. The patient was urged to give in to any impulse he might feel and on no account to fight it. The lips then began to protrude and retract rhythmically. As the treatment continued the mouth twitched and emitted sounds like painful sobbing. Then the expression changed from misery to anger. Sometimes he sat up and raised his fist threateningly only to fall back whimpering.

So far there was a divorce between the outward signs of rage and the subjective feeling. Although he behaved as though in the grip of strong emotions, he was actually detached. This detachment disappeared, however, when he remembered an older brother who used to bully him when he was a child. He admitted that he had hated his brother, who had been his mother's favourite, and he understood that he had repressed his hatred and over-compensated by appearing to be affectionate.

Reich was pleased with his progress. He had brought out the repressed hatred by the action of the muscles instead of by free association. The older analytical technique produced a memory to which there was an emotional response. This new technique excites muscular (vegetative) activity, which then brings back the memory of an earlier situation and in this case jealousy of an older brother.

The treatment, it should be noted, consisted of daily sessions and lasted six and a half months. After Reich had dealt with facial expression, the patient reported twitchings in the chest and new sensations in the abdomen which spread to the legs but not to the pelvis. Some of the spasms were so violent that they almost resembled epilepsy. Yet the patient still remained essentially detached although he found the twitching of his legs pleasurable.

More clues were dredged from the past in regard to the extreme caution the patient displayed. He suddenly remembered that when he was a small boy his mother caught him playing on the brink of a dangerous cliff. She coaxed him to go to her by promising sweets. When he did so she gave him a severe beating. This experience made a lasting impression and he acknowledged that it might have some connection with his defensive attitude towards women.

During one session when his body jerked very vigorously he said he felt like a fish. Reich had already noticed an odd resemblance between the way his body threshed about and the protruding, twisted mouth and a fish caught on the line. To Reich this meant that after the treatment he had received from his mother, frequent beatings and neglect, he trusted no one. He didn't want to be caught, hence his caution, his fear of giving himself to a woman, his spontaneous acting out the part of a trout that had taken the bait.

The final breakthrough came in a session when he acted the part of a sucking infant. His lips went through the appropriate movements and he was seized by a sudden anxiety. He felt threatened by an approaching animal and then remembered an incident at the age of two when he saw a picture of a gorilla. "Don't be angry, I only want to suck", he cried out. The gorilla is interpreted as representing his father.

The infantile conflict with the father developed as a desire to be independent and yet at the same time to be protected. The latter he associated with femininity. He had been conditioned by upbringing to believe that to be masculine is to be hard and that any kind of surrender is feminine. Towards the end of the therapy he met a young, attractive woman and most of the inhibitions that had previously spoiled any sexual relationship disappeared. He told Reich with surprise and pride that his pelvis had moved "so peculiarly by itself". It was not long before the last obstacle was removed—the resistance to allowing his neck to relax. Once he did so the somewhat jerky contractions of the pelvis gave place to the smooth, harmonious movements of an unimpeded orgasm reflex.

Importance of Respiration

It was in treating this patient that Reich came to realize the importance of breathing technique. He found the combined pressures of the diaphragm and abdominal wall on the solar plexus were factors in maintaining the character armour. With deep expiration of breath sensations of pleasure are felt in the abdomen; but the function of a respiratory block, i.e. reducing the depth of exhalation, is to prevent these sensations from occurring. The sensations are, of course, sexual, and this is why the neurotic fears them. What he really fears is the experience of letting himself go. Holding the breath ensures that he holds himself in control of himself.

Reich appeals to the common experience in childhood of competing to see who can hold his breath longest. Most people have played some such game. The swimmer who could stay under water the longest was always admired. Holding the breath was equated with self-control, and what could be more heroic than supreme feats of self-control? Many of Reich's patients who felt pleasurable abdominal sensations took fright because they had been conditioned to believe that they must never lose control.

He mentions one patient who was exhaling deeply on the couch with the result that there was marked sensitivity in the pelvic region. He promptly reacted by holding his breath and effectively killed the sensation. From then on, the work was concentrated on having the patient give a detached description of his behaviour in the sexual act.

The Theory of Vegetotherapy

It is difficult to see how by encouraging a patient to be self-conscious about the sexual act he can be led to behave entirely involuntarily at the climax. It is possible that the self-observation is a necessary part of the treatment, but it must obviously cease when the treatment comes to a successful conclusion. Once the muscular inhibitions have been dissolved the body takes over as a whole. The differently located blockages—in the throat, chest, abdomen, pelvis—have been attacked one by one until finally the impulses of the body are integrated in a harmonious unity.

The theory of vegetotherapy is that the Unconscious is located in the para-sympathetic nervous system which gives rise to pleasure, as distinct from the sympathetic system which gives rise to anxiety and anger. Both these systems are the source of involuntary autonomic behaviour.

Reich sought to reduce all biological impulses to the fundamental functions of expansion and contraction. In pleasure the heart expands, the peripheral blood-vessels dilate, the skin reddens and the musculature is relaxed. In anxiety, the heart contracts and beats faster to drive the blood through constricted blood vessels. The skin shows pallor, the secretion of saliva is decreased, the musculature is paralysed. Reich co-relates the para-sympathetic "expansion" with a psychological "going out" from the narrow confines of the ego to the world in life-affirming activity. On the other hand, the sympathetic system governs a process in the opposite direction, a "contraction" which in psychological language is a withdrawal from the external world back into the Self.

This is an interesting speculation and we can see why Reich frowned upon certain Eastern ideas which seem superficially to have much in common with his own. Yoga exercises, for example, also reverse the technique of influencing the body by changing the state of the mind, and endeavour to influence the mind through the body. Extreme importance is attached to posture. Even more is expected from correct breathing. But the parallels are misleading. Most Yoga training produces the very opposite result to that which vegetotherapy aims at. The Yogi withdraws from the world into an introverted serenity. He strives to be detached from sexual desire, whereas Reich's goal is the perfect orgasm.

There are, indeed, some kinds of Yoga which, as the erotic art of India shows, do not advocate abstinence. But the form of sexual activity recommended is the kind known as Karezza, and this is anathema to Reich. Karezza—sometimes called *coitus reservatus*—means that the penis remains in the vagina without ejaculating. It was partially based on false theory that loss of semen is weakening.

Reich's view of the effects of shallow breathing is scarcely less mistaken, though it may have been considered pragmatic justification. He maintained that shallow breathing, more especially poor exhalation, is a defence mechanism used by neurotics to reduce their vitality by breathing in less oxygen. The less energy available, the easier breathing is to control. The inhibition of respiration is therefore one way of reducing anxiety. One can only remark that if that is the object it is singularly unsuccessful.

The dogmatic assertion that no neurotic can exhale deeply and evenly would be more significant if it were not applicable to almost everyone. To argue from this that everyone is neurotic may be true in the trivial sense that nobody can claim absolute mental health, but the more all-embracing the statement the more its usefulness is watered down.

Yet there is a connection between breathing and anxiety. Breathing troubles, muscular tension and neurotic conditions are closely interwoven. In applying vegetotherapy Reich urged the patient to exhale deeply. Continued strong exhalations sometimes had startling effects. One method was for the analyst to press with fingertips below the sternum. A typical neurotic reaction would be to arch the back and pull back the pelvis as a defence against sexual excitation. In other cases pressure of the hand would cause rippling contractions in the abdomen, sometimes spreading lower and becoming orgastic. Perhaps this is not altogether surprising when such a dynamic personality as Reich touched the patient lying on the couch, urging him (or her) to "give in" completely.

Vegetotherapy is based on the theory that every muscular rigidity contains the history of its origin. Character can not only be read in the facial expression but in the whole body. The emotional past is there in cipher, but only the psychiatrist who possesses the key can read it. He need not keep strictly to a physical technique. How far to combine muscle therapy with character analysis depends on the individual patient. Instead of following the Freudian practice of telling the patient to say anything that occurs to him, Reich felt he could gain more understanding by treating the way a patient spoke, looked, walked and sat as a means of unintentional communication. Even his silence could be revealing.

The goal was not merely to cure certain neurotic symptoms but to integrate the personality and produce a condition of joyous inner freedom. The process of liberation involved a release of powerful suppressed emotions. A striking example of this occurred in Reich's early experience when a patient came out of a stupor in a sudden violent discharge of aggression. When his rage spent itself he declared that the explosion had been a euphoric experience. Reich could not explain this behaviour on the psychoanalytic theory of catatonia.

The muscular spasms induced by vegetotherapy are explosive. They are not unlike the convulsions brought about in a Voodoo trance, or in the once common phenomenon of Christian exorcism. This is a wide and insufficiently explored territory. Reich throws some light on the relief, sometimes sheer ecstasy, which follows the discharge of suppressed emotion through the body. But although a completely satisfying sexual life is essential to fulfilment, it cannot be the only goal worth pursuing.

Reich's own life was a long and tormented pursuit of knowledge. The same may be said of many scientists who live for their work and for whom sex is of lesser importance. Equally, many of the greatest creative artists had stormy and not always satisfying sexual experiences. Many were homosexual—a condition which Reich regarded as neurotic.

He was altogether too drastic in dismissing all forms of sexual activity but one as neurotic. It has not been established that there is only one correct type of orgasm. Many people enjoy sex in ways that are very different from that prescribed by Reich, and they are not troubled by guilt or anxiety. Many more do not even enjoy sex because they are worrying about the quality of their orgasm.

When allowance is made for Reich's exaggerations and a single-mindedness amounting to monomania, his real contribution has been grossly underestimated. The idea that character is a form of defence, and that it can be read from the state of the musculature, is much more fruitful than some of the deviations from Freud. Reich was a pioneer of psychsomatic medicine and this may prove to be his most lasting achievement.

6 Sexuality and Love

The controversy over sex education in Britain in the summer of 1971 recalls the even more bitter storms aroused some forty years earlier when Reich advanced ideas similar to those of Dr. Martin Cole, a lecturer in genetics, who was responsible for a film "Growing up", intended for schools. Dr. Cole declared that the assumption that sex can only be taught as part of "a loving relationship" is dishonest. This is an endeavour to hide from children the truth about their own sexuality—"to de-sexualize sex". If this film encouraged teenagers to be promiscuous, he thought this to be a good thing. Promiscuity in adolescence is a "learning situation" and possibly helpful for children who are emotionally deprived.

Reich was a powerful advocate of sexual freedom in adolescence, and he, too, was sparing in his use of the word "love". Thus he speaks of "the capacity to love or sexual potency" as though they are synonymous. Teenagers who do not have sexual intercourse as soon as they are capable were said to be victims of parental tyranny. The courageous ones rebel; the rest are submissive and without ambition. The romantic agony so characteristic of this age presumably owes its intensity to unrelieved tension.

The only way in which tension can be completely relieved, on this view, is by sexual intercourse. And according to Reich there is only one way to get total satisfaction in intercourse. The climax must be the type of orgasm he has described—or should we say, prescribed? Those who fail to reach perfection are neurotic. In an irrational society this is the fate of most people, unless they are fortunate enough to be treated by vegetotherapy or to live in the primitive simplicity of South Sea Islanders.

It is all very logical but it demands a self-consistency seldom found in real life. In the present social conditions, to encourage sexual intercourse at the age of fifteen is surely dangerous without the assurance that contraception will be used. When Reich wrote, less was known about contraception than today, but in any case it is not merely a question of knowledge. Surveys show that in a high proportion of unwanted pregnancies adults took no precautions whatever, though they could not plead ignorance. Is it likely that schoolchildren will exercise more care than grown-ups?

As for any love-making that falls short of intercourse, Reich condemned it as neurotic. With the relentless persistence of an *idée fixe* he insists that "orgastic potency" is the proper goal if we wish for a healthy organism. It is only in the orgasm reflex that sexual energy is wholly discharged. A partial discharge leaves a residue which must find other employment.

Salvation through Sex

Reich follows an early idea of Freud's that undischarged libido is converted into anxiety. If it is not used to give pleasure, it yields the opposite, unpleasure. But there are two alternatives. Instead of creating anxiety, a partial discharge may activate infantile fantasies, religious mysticism or other systems of thought. Or the undischarged energy may be transformed into sadism. Reich also believed that the repressed wish for orgasm continues to seek satisfaction, and as this is denied it results in a feeling of aggression. Turned into sexual channels aggression leads to sadistic or masochistic activities.

Reich emphasized that orgasm, therefore, is man's only salvation, leading us to the Kingdom of Heaven on earth. Those who enjoy it are no longer trapped in the rat-race for power or money. Their lives are richer than they had previously thought possible. They are healthy physically as well as mentally because so many diseases are psychosomatic.

These are somewhat dazzling claims to base on a single bodily function. Some over-statement is understandable in view of the emotional resistance always encountered to a liberal attitude to sex. But there are questions still to be asked even by those broadly in sympathy with Reich's outlook. Why, for example, must we suppose that the *only* way sexual energy can be successfully discharged is in orgastic union? Is it really true that homosexuals and lesbians do not experience orgasm? Is it not reached by lovers who for some reason must practise deep petting; Indeed, can the energy be discharged only through genital activity? There are cases in which a rush of spontaneous joy, the sight of some beautiful scene, the sound of music, produce physical sensations and breathlessness that have a great deal in common with orgasm.

Reich would no doubt reply that energy only partly released leaves a residue which at best could be used up in mysticism or at the worst in the violence of destructiveness displayed, for example, by Fascism. He assumes the validity of Freud's early model of psychic structure, which pictures forces of attraction and repulsion circulating among the ideas and impulses located in the ego, the Super-ego and the Id. Although referred to as though they had spatial position, this is a heuristic device for the sake of convenience. By using what is a "useful fiction" we can speak of impulses being *below* the conscious level, as though the instinctual forces of the Id were in some underground compartment.

The Conscious and Unconscious form an energy system, the sexual aspect of which was called *libido* by Freud. He was as convinced as Reich that mental energy had a bodily origin, but in orthodox psychoanalysis this has a more theoretical than practical significance. Reich, on the other hand, believed that libido was an objective substance. It could be detected by instruments and actually seen.

Temporary and Permanent Relationships

Reich's outlook is so "physicalistic" that in dealing with sexual relationships he seldom needs to use the word "love". He seems to judge their success more by somatic standards than by the quality of feeling. Instead of speaking of a love affair, he nearly always refers to a "sexual relationship". He does, however, admit the importance of a "tender attitude", though he does not think this becomes strong until a certain gratification of sexual needs has taken place.

It is a matter of ordinary observation that some people develop a more mature affection for each other after they have cohabited for a period. It is this possibility that makes arranged marriages often more successful than those based on romantic love.

Reich is scornful of conventional marriage and prefers to classify sexual relationships as either lasting or temporary. By lasting he does not mean life-long, unless the partners genuinely wish to make it so, which he seems to think rather unlikely. And by temporary he means anything from one hour to as long as it lasts.

Temporary relationships are likely to lack the tenderness which is present in a long-lasting relationship. Because there is insufficient time for the partners to adjust to each other the sexual satisfaction is not so complete as in a more stable situation. That is not to imply that transient relationships are worthless, or, as the moralists would argue, that they are intrinsically wrong.

The capacity for a permanent sexual relationship, we are told, presupposes: (1) Full orgastic potency; (2) the overcoming of incestuous fixation and infantile sexual anxiety; (3) the absence of repression of any unsublimated sexual strivings, be they homosexual or non-genital; (4) absolute affirmation of sexuality and *joie de vivre*. This is a formidable list, and Reich adds the warning that none of the requirements can be met in an authoritarian society, except by a few individuals.

It might be thought that the fortunate *élite* who are able to satisfy these conditions will be rewarded by an ideal partnership for the rest of their lives. Not so; "permanent" should read "long-lasting" and how long depends on individual circumstances. "The basic difficulty of any permanent sexual relationship is the conflict between dulling (temporary or final) of sensual desire on the one hand and the increasing tender attachment to the partner on the other hand." (*The Sexual Revolution*, p. 123.)

So love—if we may use the word—instead of resolving the conflict, intensifies it. There is an astringent realism in this analysis of the situation. Those living in legal wedlock may seem to solve their problems, but they only succeed in suppressing them. Conventional marriage is held together by the moralistic outlook of society. A man or woman (or both) may long to escape from the monotony of their sex life and seek new experience, but they fear public opinion or the economic hardship of breaking-up.

Sufficiently sophisticated people may frankly recognize the difficulty and consent to an experiment. Even so it is hardly impossible to avoid feeling jealous of the rival. Reich points out that the real harm of jealousy is only when it becomes possessive. Most people today would agree that the existence of a marriage certificate does not magically protect either partner from the wish to be unfaithful.

Nature knows nothing of either monogamy or polygamy, it only knows that all through life powerful sexual impulses persist in every healthy individual. They can be suppressed but they cannot be ignored. Frustration acts like a slow poison. What began as love turns into its opposite. Paradoxically, hate is often masked by an increasing show of outward affection. This is a typical over-compensation because of the guilty longing to be unfaithful. In the end, however, two people who continue to live together, despite a mounting frustration, cannot keep up a pretence indefinitely. They grow farther and farther apart until they are virtually strangers.

Extra-marital Relationships

All this misery could have been avoided, Reich contends, if they had accepted a relationship with a third person, at least for a trial period. If that does not work out the restless desire for novelty will be cured—for a time, anyhow. A woman, for example, who is bored with the sexual routine of marriage, should be able to take a lover with the full knowledge of her husband, or vice versa. The result may well be disappointing. In that case, they should be able to resume their normal married life without hard feelings. The mutual understanding they have gained should deepen their affection. The cure for an unhappy marriage is often infidelity.

But suppose it does not end on such a happy note. Very often one partner wants his freedom and the other does not. In a sense this is an insoluble problem because the wishes of both are incompatible. The worst thing would be for the two to remain together out of a sense of duty, or because of public opinion. This would merely built up a resentment possibly amounting to hatred.

Reich is not very hopeful of any union succeeding for a long period whether or not it is a formal marriage. It stands a better chance if both partners have enjoyed sexual freedom in adolescence and are emancipated from conventional morality. Yet this very emancipation makes it almost impossible for them to establish a permanent relationship, unless they accept each other's right to have other sexual experiences. Four years is probably as long as they can be content without a change.

In a masculine-dominated society it is much easier for a married man to have love affairs than for a woman. A man finds it hard to accept his wife's sexual freedom for a number of reasons. Socially a "cuckold" is despised, but a woman who is deceived is more likely to be pitied. Unless she is courageous enough, and sufficiently independent economically, she may suffer from sexual stasis and frigidity.

Although Reich inveighed against a double standard of morality, he was not quite free from it himself. According to his wife he was extremely jealous and on one occasion after she had been away on a long vacation he put her through a third-degree questioning. "He asked me especially whether I had been faithful to him during those two months. I almost had to take an oath of fidelity before he would be satisfied. Of course, I knew about his jealousy, but I found at that time a moralistic attitude in him such as he usually attacked in others. The double standard of sexual behaviour was quite apparent in his attack. I was not allowed to question his faithfulness to me during that period, but I was quite certain that he did not apply to himself the same standards he expected of me. In fact I knew he had had an affair although he did not tell me so." (*William Reich: A Personal Biography* by Ilse Ollendorff Reich, Paul Elek, 1969, p. 82.)

The Meaning of Love

A personal inconsistency does not invalidate the argument. But there are several objections to Reich's views on personal relationships. I do not think we need deny the value of much that he has to say, but it is of limited application. It is limited because it restricts the meaning of love to orgasm, and orgasm to a special kind of reflex.

What love means apart from sexual intercourse is never explained. Reich does not deny that a man and woman may feel affection for each other out of bed, but he doesn't seem to find this very interesting. At least, that is the impression he gives.

This is not to belittle the value of the type of orgasm he describes with a detailed accuracy that is remarkable when we recall that he wrote over forty years ago. He is perfectly entitled to say "That is how I choose to define orgasm", but he should not deny the freedom of other psychologists to define it more broadly.

One is reminded of the futile dispute about whether there is a qualitative difference between clitoral and vaginal orgasm. Equally, we can admit that if both partners reach their climax simultaneously the satisfaction may be more intense, without holding it up as an ideal which must be strained after at all costs. Sex can be sufficiently satisfying when this does not occur, and if Reich stigmatizes whatever falls short of his own account of orgasm as "neurotic", all he is doing is to define "neurotic" as failure to reach full orgasm, which is to argue in a circle.

It is significant that he attaches great importance to a solemn approach to the sex act. Neither partner must laugh, and it is advisable not to speak, except perhaps for a few words of endearment. Tenderness is then used as a means to an end. This is not so much love as a form of love-play, for its object is sexual arousal to intercourse.

If a deep relationship satisfies the sexual needs completely, we may well ask why should it come to pall? Why does the "genital character" find that after a time even the experience of "orgastic potency" with the same partner loses its original power? According to Reich every sexual relationship sooner or later becomes dulled. This is hardly a new discovery; yet it is puzzling, in view of Reich's theory, that it should happen to those who have lost their neurotic inhibitions and are capable of the perfect orgasm. Why should they want a change of partner? What more do they expect?

Something is missing from Reich's account. The identification of mental health with orgastic potency is too narrow to encompass the rich variety of interpersonal relationships. It is open to much the same objection as Dr. Martin Cole's fear that to talk about love may be a puritanical stratagem to de-sexualize sex. Certainly we must be wary of any playing-down of the physical reality of sex. But thanks to Freud we now know why the enjoyment of sex is not entirely focused on the genitals. Sexuality is diffused all over the body, though more sensitively in some zones than others. The gratification experienced by non-genital contacts is of great value in itself and is not a mere preliminary to intercourse.

According to Reich infantile constraint results in muscular rigidities which make the free movement of the pelvis impossible during intercourse. Undischarged sexual energy is at the core of every neurosis. Once it is discharged the individual is restored to health.

But the harm done by a faulty upbringing is not always the result of sexual prohibitions. Recent research has confirmed the belief that deprivation of love in early childhood is at least as important a factor. By love what is meant is the physical manifestation of affection by stroking, kissing and cuddling. These actions speak louder than words to an infant. He needs the overt signs that he is loved as much as he needs food. Some interesting animal experiments suggest that the comforting reassurance of bodily contact means more than food.

Tactile Stimulation

In a series of laboratory studies of monkeys Professor H. Harlow constructed two surrogate mothers, one of soft cloth warmed by an electric bulb, and the other of wire mesh. To four newborn babies milk was given from the cloth mother, and not from the wire mother; for four other babies the condition was reversed. The experiment was designed to test the importance attached to the comfort of feeding and the comfort of bodily contact. The result, says Harlow, "makes it obvious that contact comfort is a variable of overwhelming importance in the develop-

73

ment of affectional responses, whereas lactation is a variable of negligible importance. With age and opportunity to learn, subjects with the lactating wire mother showed decreasing responsiveness to her and increasing responsiveness to the non-lactating cloth mother . . ." (*Proceedings, American Philosophical Society,* No. 102, 1958, pp. 501–509.)

Anyone could have guessed that a monkey, or a human child, would prefer to snuggle against a soft, warm cloth figure rather than one of wire mesh, but few would have predicted that the pleasure of bodily contact would overshadow that of feeding. The powerful effect of these early experiences was revealed by the subsequent history of monkeys deprived of contact with a real mother. They did not show normal sexual behaviour such as posturing before they were impregnated. Towards their offspring they were either indifferent or violently abusive.

Anthropological studies show that in some communities children are in close bodily contact with the mother for a surprisingly long period. In Bali a child is carried on the hip during the day and sleeps in the mother's arms at night. Birth does not involve a traumatic severance from the mother's body. The constant availability of tactile stimulation gives a sense of security which is markedly absent in other primitive societies where a Spartan childhood is followed by an anxious and aggressive manhood.

The Samoans, like Malinowski's Trobrianders, are also tolerant and easy-going about infantile and adolescent sexuality. They are free from that puritanical conditioning which, in patriarchal societies, cripples adult sexuality, according to Reich. Margaret Mead says that they have one of the smoothest sex adjustments in the world. "In Samoa, the expected personality is one to which sex will be a delightful experience, expertly engaged in, but which will not be sufficiently engrossing to threaten the social order. The Samoans condone light love affairs but repudiate passionate choice, and have no real place for anyone who would continue, in spite of social experiences to the contrary, to prefer one woman or one man to a more socially acceptable mate." (*Male and Female,* Gollancz, 1950, p. 114.)

Whether or not they have "orgastic potency", there can be little doubt that they possess a Reichian "genital character".

They are free from any sense of guilt regarding sex, apart from a strict incest rule. By thinking of love mainly in terms of physical satisfaction they avoid the emotional storms that occur in our own society. But there is a debit side; Margaret Mead continues: "The price they pay for their smooth, even generously gratifying system is the failure to use special gifts, special intelligence, special intensity. There is no place in Samoa for the man or the woman capable of great passion, of complicated aesthetic feeling, of deep religious devotion." (*Ibid.*, p. 118.)

Sensuality and Sexuality

It would be unfair to Reich to suggest that he favoured a superficial relationship. Dr. Alexander Lowen, a disciple of Reich, accepts the identification of love and orgasm but makes a distinction between sexuality and sensuality. The former demands maturity of body and mind, whereas the sensualist is immature.

The sensualist, he contends, is fixated at the oral stage of development. Either he has been deprived of body contacts or he has had an excess of them. (How much, one wonders, is enough?) The sensual or oral personality that emerges from such an upbringing prefers a passive role and treats forepleasure as an end in itself. Fellatio and cunnilingus are often preferred substitutes for normal coition. By contrast, the sexual personality acts aggressively to get what he wants. "His life is orientated to achievement and fulfilment because he is afraid to mobilize his aggression in the service of his desire", writes Dr. Lowen. (*Love and Orgasm*, New American Library, 1965, p. 187.)

It is not very clear how the Balinese or Samoans fit into these categories. Those elements of adult sexuality which reproduce a loving mother-child relationship are as much an ingredient of a full emotional life as orgasm. The language of the body contains more than one word. It would be absurd to dismiss kissing and caressing as neurotic regressions to infancy unless they lead to intercourse.

Dr. L. K. Frank, in a monograph on Tactile Communication, writes: "But the elementary sexual processes of the human organism may be transformed and focused into an interpersonal love relationship with an identified person to whom each is seeking to communicate, using sex, not for procreation, as in the mating of a female in heat, ready to be fertilized, but as 'another language' for inter-personal communication, which has been largely overlaid and superseded by auditory and visual signs and symbols, is reinstated to function with elementary organic intensity, provided the individuals have not lost the capacity for communication with the self through tactile experiences." (Quoted by Ashley Montagu in *Touching*, Columbia University Press, 1971, p. 174.)

Most contemporary psychologists would question Reich's statement that "mental illness is a result of a disturbance in the natural capacity for love". This may often be the cause, but there are other frustrations besides sex. And by "the natural capacity for love", Reich means orgastic potency. The later development of his theory even more explicitly identified love with the energy discharged during orgasm. Love is not an idea in the head but a physical quality which, he believed, can be observed by an electroscope or a Geiger counter.

What is left out of this account is the love felt by parents and children, and the deep friendship with members of the same or opposite sex which is not dependent on orgastic satisfaction—or even necessarily capable of it. The experiments with monkeys already alluded to suggest that affection demonstrated by bodily contacts in infancy is absolutely essential to emotional maturation. We have ample evidence, too, that children deprived of love in the early years have the greatest difficulty in forming a deep adult relationship. Never having received love they do not know how to give it.

It might be thought that genital love has primacy because it is an obvious biological need. This, however, is not quite what Reich meant. Biological needs can be satisfied without orgasm, since it should be remembered that for Reich coitus is not the same as "orgastic potency". From a biological standpoint orgasm is a luxury. The species could be very well maintained without it, and that is the present situation, if Reich is correct in thinking that most people do not experience true orgasm.

There is no point in asking which is the more important, non-genital or genital love. In a mature personality there is no conflict between them. We may agree with Reich that a child whose sexual growth is distorted by unnatural prohibitions will find it difficult, and probably impossible, to establish a satisfying sexual relationship later on. But the same is equally true of a child deprived of love. It is possible that to be denied love is even more serious. The capacity for love, whether or not it always shows itself in genital sex, is an index of mental health.

Its enormous significance as a force for social good conduct cannot be exaggerated. The opposite of love is hate. Reich's views on the origins of hate and sadism marked a further deviation from Freudian orthodoxy. They have an appeal today to sections of the New Left which have more in common with anarchism than Soviet Communism.

7 Enemies of Freedom

A happy life for the majority of mankind is impossible unless the power of religion is broken, Reich contended in *The Mass Psychology of Fascism*. Religion is the instrument used to impose an anti-sexual morality on the masses. It is the great enemy of human freedom. It's deadly influence is used as a substitute for sexuality.

Yet why should people prefer a substitute? There is little in the orthodox teaching—i.e. of Christianity—to explain its extraordinarily powerful hold on the minds of men. It prohibits the most natural of pleasures, and threatens those who break its commandments with dreadful punishments. The fear of hell is implanted in the mind of the child, and, even when that ceases to be believed in consciously, the anxiety may still lurk in the unconscious. One thing is certain : sex life is poisoned at the source.

Since Reich framed this passionate indictment there has been a marked decline in religion and a corresponding increase in sexual permissiveness which may seem to prove his point. But it is easy to overestimate the extent of the change outside urban and sophisticated circles. The puritanical attitude in totalitarian countries, where religion is attacked and the Establishment is atheistic, is as rigorous as ever. And this shows that religion is not by any means the sole determining factor.

Reich was still too much of a Marxist to make such a claim. If, instead of religion, we use the wider term ideology, his argument is stronger. Ideology is a reflection in men's minds of the power structure of the society to which they belong, according to Marx. Its function is to support the structure, to find reasons for submitting to it.

The old idea of the Divine Right of Kings is a somewhat crude instance of a religious doctrine being used to justify the privileges of the ruling class. It appeared in a more disguised form as the duty each individual held to keep to the station in life to which it had pleased God to call him. When this was eroded by the growth of democracy, all that remained was the idea that the social order in some sense must be consonant with the will of God.

The False Consciousness

"Ideology", wrote Engels, "is a process which of course is carried on with the consciousness of so-called thinkers, but with a *false* consciousness. The real driving force which moves it remains unconscious. Otherwise it would not be an ideological process." (Translated by Sidney Hook in *Towards the Understanding of Karl Marx*, Gollancz, 1933, p. 282.)

This concept of a "false consciousness" providing reasons for behaviour which has in fact a very different and unacknowledged motivation is similar to the Freudian concept of rationalization. But an ideology is not the rationalization in one individual mind for purely personal motives. It embraces the beliefs and ideals in many individual minds which are derived from the traditions of society. We are born into a society in which certain assumptions about right and wrong, the existence of God, duty to the State, are taken for granted. Within such a framework to doubt them is either blasphemy or sedition, or both.

Reich knew from bitter experience what it meant to defy the current orthodoxy, even in countries like Scandinavia and the United States, which pride themselves on free speech. The conclusion he drew was that all orthodoxies serve the interests of the dominant class. The ideological superstructure is a function of the social structure, just as rationalizations in individual consciousness are functions of unconscious drives.

The strong emotional appeal of religion is not wholly explained by its sociological function as a preserver of the *status quo*, but at least the existence of an unconscious motivation enables us to understand why highly intelligent people cling to beliefs that seem to so many to be absurd. Thus such a towering intellect as Newton was fascinated all his life by studying the prophecies of Daniel. It would be easy to multiply instances. Many who give up the faith of their childhood nevertheless retain a lingering nostalgia and feel they must have lost something precious.

As Reich points out, the lack of success of free-thought propaganda plainly shows that religion is much more than an intellectual mistake. A believer may lose all the arguments and be completely unaffected. He has what William James called "the will to believe", and although this is partly wishful thinking, we still have to account for the wish that God should prohibit pleasure. This takes us back to the feelings of guilt and shame experienced in childhood.

Infantile masturbation and any subsequent interest in sex are repressed in the average patriarchal family. Sexual pleasure is sinful, except under certain stringent conditions which greatly diminish the pleasure. It would be difficult to clamp down such a powerful drive as sex without using fear as a weapon. For a young child summary punishment is enough to create an inhibition. Later, in addition to physical punishment and warnings of black disgrace, religion threatens the wrath of God. All this amounts to the most effective brainwashing imaginable.

If the victim of this psychological technique gives up religion when he is older, he may still have been crippled by his early training. He may then go to the opposite extreme and wallow in "the sins of the flesh" in a restless search for the full satisfaction he can never find. On the other hand, if he becomes extremely religious he will look for compensation in subjective experiences. If his religious education has been successful he will be unable to relieve sexual tension in any normal way; consequently his hopes turn to happiness in the next world as a reward for his self-denial here and now.

Sexual Mysticism

"Mystical feelings", says Reich, are "at one and the same time anti-sexual and a substitute for sexuality." He supports this view by referring to patients he has treated and to the lives and writings of mystics. It cannot be a coincidence that the Catholic Church has placed great emphasis on celibacy for priests and members of religious orders. The same requirement is found in many other religions. Buddha abandoned his wife and children and preached the suppression of desire as a means to Nirvana. In our own time Mahatma Gandhi gave up married life and tested his self-control by sleeping with young girls, a practice known to the early Christian Church as *syneisaktism* or spiritual marriage.

Not all religions are other-worldly. Judaism is not preoccupied by the thought of life after death and it is free of the anti-sex bias of the ascetic religions. The latter are based on sexual repression and the anxiety this produces. If it is asked why people should choose to burden themselves with a religion of self-denial, Reich's answer is that a mature adult would not make this choice. In most cases it is made for him in childhood when religious instruction is part of the curriculum in schools as well as being reinforced in the home background.

Moreover, there are transient rewards for abstinence. The mystics are visited with an occasional experience of ecstasy which is not unlike sexual excitement. The search for this sense of union with God—sometimes depicted in erotic language as the embrace of the Bride and divine Bridegroom—is brusquely dismissed by Reich as the "illusory happiness provided by the religious fore-pleasure excitations".

If rationalist propaganda is too intellectualist to counter these irrational forces, the question remains of what else can be done. Reich faces the problem quite realistically. The Russian experience convinced him that a purely political revolution is unlikely to be extended into a moral revolution, since it is necessarily carried out by adults whose attitude has already been warped by early training. The economic structure can be changed overnight but not the psychic structure.

Any hope of a sudden transformation must be given up. Progress towards liberalization is possible in course of time only through new educational methods. Reich's extremely radical views on sex education evoke little surprise today. Feeding by the clock and strict toilet training are no longer in favour, even among those who would not go so far as Reich to encourage infantile masturbation and adolescent sexual freedom.

He believed that the tide was already turning in favour of greater permissiveness and that Western society was in the midst of a "deep-reaching revolution of cultural living" in which "the senses of the animal, man, for his natural life functions are awakening from a sleep of thousands of years". It was not brought about by propaganda but as the inevitable outcome of social changes. Women, after the First World War, were beginning to work alongside men in factories and offices and the professions. By gaining more economic independence women became less tied to the home and family. Easier divorce laws would still further hasten the break-up of traditional marriage.

Religion was the chief obstacle to a cultural revolution which, unlike the Russian Revolution, was "without parades, uniforms, drums or cannon salutes". The Churches must therefore be deprived of "their evil right of preparing children's minds for the reception of reactionary ideologies". It was religious indoctrination at this level that maimed the growing child and substituted the illusory excitation of mysticism for the natural fulfilment of sexuality.

Reich's prescience must be acknowledged whether or not one entirely agrees with his attitude. He foresaw the disintegration of the old sexual morality, which has only recently reached obviously a point of no return. It is unthinkable that the pendulum will again swing back to a rigorous puritanizing, in spite of the efforts of the Churches to halt the trend.

The Upbringing of Children

It would be a gross travesty of Reich's crusade against "Moralism" to suppose that he advocated a "free for all". He explains his views on the upbringing of children with such frankness that the editor of a pedagogic journal which printed them was sent to prison. By today's standards they would still shock many people, as the furore caused by Dr. Martin Cole has shown. The aim of sex-education is simply the creation of a "life-affirming" attitude instead of one that is "life-negating". If this sounds too vague and grandiose, what it means is plainly indicated.

Children, we are told, should be allowed to discover for themselves that sexuality is something to be enjoyed. None of its early manifestations should be forbidden, including the perfectly natural curiosity which makes a child want to *see* nudity and *watch* lovemaking. To deny these impulses can only be justified by appealing to the old morality which is so psychologically injurious.

Early sexual drives are repressed as a rule by parents. The child looks upon them as the repositories of authority. From time to time he may rebel, but if he has developed a parent fixation he will still feel that authority is part of the natural order. Any act of defiance is likely to produce an emotional conflict. The situation is worse if the fixation has become unconscious, as it may then release sexual interests by a pathological compromise between sexuality and guilt. The basis of psychological health cannot be laid unless the parental fixation is dissolved.

The possibility that pre-marital intercourse may be more likely to lead to extra-marital intercourse does not trouble Reich. He welcomes it. Since then various surveys show that women who lost their virginity before marriage are more ready to accept extra-marital relationships than those who had been abstinent.

"Abstinence is dangerous and absolutely harmful to health", Reich writes. "The suppressed sexual energy expresses itself in different ways. Either, a nervous disturbance appears very soon, or the adolescent begins to indulge in daydreams; these interfere seriously with his work. True, those who refuse to see the connection between sexual excitation and nervous disorders may easily say that abstinence is not harmful or that it is practicable in most cases. They only see that the adolescent does live in abstinence and conclude that, therefore, it is practicable." He continues that it is often overlooked "that a tendency to protracted abstinence is in itself already a pathological symptom, indicating rather complete repression of conscious sexual desire. It always—sooner or later—damages the love life and reduces achievement in work." (*The Sexual Revolution*, p. 107.)

Repression and Cultural Achievement

Freud held that sexual energy could be diverted from its original goal and used creatively in social and cultural achievements. This mechanism was termed sublimation, though it does not apply solely to sexual instincts. Homicidal impulses can also be directed into safe channels by refining and reversing their aims. For example: a man might become a writer of thrillers,

83

a student of war, or even a surgeon. Sexual impulses can be similarly deflected from their biological aim to relationships based on non-sensual friendship. A frustration which might otherwise lead to anxiety gives rise through sublimation to a different sort of pleasure. The drive of personal ambition, the lure of power, devotion to some great cause, are some of the possible ways of sublimating the libidinal instincts. The implication of this view of sublimation was that most of the higher developments of civilization are the result of instinctual repression.

Art and invention, it has been argued, could not have arisen if primitive man had been content to satisfy his instincts and dream away his life like the lotus-eaters. The "noble savage" of Rousseau, who made such an appeal to Reich, has his counterpart in the South Seas—e.g. the Trobrianders—but if mankind had remained at that level there would be no great poetry or painting or sculpture or music or science of any kind.

This is flatly denied by Reich, though he offers no evidence to the contrary. On his own theory it is difficult to see how any evidence could exist, since hardly anybody is capable of "orgastic potency" in civilized countries. Great geniuses have nearly all been neurotic, at least on Reich's definition, and their creativity has been born from their conflicts.

On the importance of sublimation Freud is more convincing than Reich. Genital satisfaction cannot be the supreme goal in life, nor is Reich entitled to say there is only one form of expression which it can take. The alternative to the type of orgasm Reich preached with almost fanatical fervour is not total celibacy, and not, to use his favourite phrase, "sexual misery". There is no point to go to the opposite extreme and claim that our culture is solely moulded and due to sexual repression. There are many other types of frustration besides sex. Alienation and lack of recognition can leave deep scars on the personality. So, above all, does lack of love—and love can be manifested in ways that have no direct sexual connotation.

The Death Instinct

The majority of psychoanalysts did not accept Freud's later theory of the Death Instinct, though they are not all in agree-

ment with Reich's criticisms. The controversy discloses a fundamental cleavage in psychological theories of which the question
of a Death Instinct is only a part. The dispute is ultimately
about whether anti-social impulses are biologically given or
whether they are the product of the environment. One school
of thought today holds that aggression is natural to man and that
the basic goodness of human nature is a myth. Genetics is cited
in support. War has been called "Nature's pruning-hook". In
The Future of an Illusion Freud declared war to be "inevitable
and indeed biologically useful".

A good deal of confusion is caused by loosely regarding aggression as synonymous with hate. If love is opposed to hate it seems
plausible to think of love as good and hate as bad. But aggression
is not always bad. Ethology has many examples of the value of
aggression in the service, not of the sex instinct, but of self-
preservation.

The latter appears to have primacy over the sex instinct. Many
animals establish the rights over a piece of territory and will
fight to maintain it. Territorial rights would seem to be as important as the sexual drive. Human beings, alas, will wage war
over a strip of territory that may in itself be almost worthless.
But the individual combatants have no wish for death. They do
not even hate the enemy, except in so far as their feelings are
worked upon by propaganda.

Both Reich and Freud attempt to reduce the dynamism of
the psyche to pairs of opposite forces. But Reich's "Life-affirming"
is narrower than Freud's *Eros* or Life instinct, since it has a
primary genital goal. Similarly, Freud's Death Instinct, or *Thanatos*, is more comprehensive that Reich's "Life-denying" principle. The latter is not an instinct at all, but a socially conditioned
attitude.

Although Freud's polarization has met with considerable
criticism, even among his followers, it was a bold attempt to
provide a philosophical frame in which the concepts of psychology
could be seen in their proper relations. As he is so often misunder-
stood, here is what Freud himself says in a summary of his final
views. "After long doubts and vacillations we have decided to
assume the existence of only two basic instincts, Eros and the

Destructive instinct. (The contrast between the instincts of self-preservation and of the preservation of the species, as well as the contrast between ego-love and object-love fall within the bounds of Eros.) The aim of the first of these basic instincts is to establish even greater unities and to preserve them thus—in short, to bind together; the aim of the second, on the contrary, is to undo connections and so destroy things. We may suppose that the final aim of the destructive instinct is to reduce living things to an inorganic state." (*An Outline of Psycho-Analysis*, The Hogarth Press, 1949, p. 6.)

The Death Instinct is seen as part of the Order of Nature. On the physical plane it can be compared with the one-way increase of entropy—the idea that the universe is running down like a cosmic clock and ultimately all change will cease. Biologically it means that there is a fundamental tendency to seek a repetition of an earlier state which has been disturbed by unsought stimuli. We do not seek food or sex for their own sakes but because we want to return to the peace which these urges interrupted. The cessation of all stimuli to which we unconsciously gravitate is death. Aggression, whether directed outward to other people or inward on ourselves, as in masochism or in suicide, is thus an innate drive.

Tragic View of Life

Freud's neglect of sociological factors is a serious weakness. In so far as he considered social circumstances, as in *Civilisation and its Discontents*, he was led to pessimistic conclusions. He treated the desire to destroy as a basic instinct and ignored the fact that in man, as in many other species, there is also an instinct of co-operation. Without the capacity to live together in communities, *Homo sapiens* could never have survived the rigours of the Ice Age, and probably would not have lasted until then. It was partly Adler's conviction that "social feeling" was the best solvent of neurotic conflicts that led to his breakaway from psychoanalysis. More recently, neo-Freudians like Harry Stack Sullivan, Karen Horney and Erich Fromm, also stress the importance of cultural rather than biological factors. In this they are in sympathy with Reich. They differ from him in holding that sexual behaviour is determined by character, not character by sexual behaviour.

Freud was not interested in trying to bring about great social changes. He did not believe that much would come of the efforts of reformers or revolutionaries. His final concept of the Death Instinct crowns his fundamentally tragic view of life. By contrast Reich was an ebullient optimist and invented a theory accordingly. He believed that it was possible to make a better world because there were no intrinsic obstacles. But his idea that the main obstacle is a chronic lack of sexual satisfaction has met with as much scepticism as Freud's Death Instinct.

If he had advanced the more moderate claim that sexual happiness is an important factor in mental health instead of insisting that it was the *only* factor, he would not have met with such opposition, though admittedly it would not have been very original. His originality was to claim that no ordinary orgasm was sufficient; it must be a very special kind of orgasm which hardly anyone, we are told, is able to experience, and consequently the evidence is meagre.

Reich's most valuable contribution to psychology is his emphasis on the part played in society in moulding not only an individual's beliefs but also his character. Man is a social product. He can no more escape completely from the traditions of the society in which he was nurtured than a fish can leave the water. Hence the hope of the future lies less in changing adult attitudes than in drastically reforming the educational system.

After 1934 Reich was disowned by orthodox psychoanalysts and Communists. It may be that he felt he had nothing more to add to psychiatric theory. His interests turned in another direction. He hoped to realize the ambition, which Freud regretfully abandoned, of establishing a neurophysiological basis for psychology. This meant turning away from analysis and pursuing the research in a laboratory with physical instruments. He came to believe that he had discovered a new kind of energy, a non-electro-magnetic force which permeates all Nature. Even his closest friends found it difficult, if not impossible, to follow him on this eccentric path.

8 Where Reich Failed

The best evidence that other frustrations besides sex lead to mental illness is provided by Reich's own experience. He believed he had made a scientific discovery of immense significance. He called it another "Copernican Revolution". But the Scientific Establishment would not consider it. He tried to console himself with the reflection that many scientific discoveries from Galileo to Freud had met with the same fate. What rankled was, not so much that he was disbelieved, but that he was ignored by those whose opinion he would have most valued.

In 1939, the year Freud died, Reich claimed to have found experimental proof of a new type of radiation. This was the culmination of a line of research he had begun in Oslo. Under a microscope he had watched the behaviour of minute vesicles which he named bions. They propagated like bacteria, and his critics declared that they were in fact bacteria which had entered through lack of stringent precautions. Bions are said to be charged with a vastly slower form of energy than that of electro-magetic waves. This is caused by orgone, a cosmic energy pervading the atmosphere which charges the cells of every living organism. Orgone energy is of two kinds. One form is mobile, without mass but occupying space, a primordial ocean of energy which moves the stars as well as the growth of living things. Orgone energy is discharged during orgasm and is the material aspect of love.

It is too easy to scoff at the idea of physical energy, tangible enough to be detected by instruments, being functionally identical with love. Poets have expressed a similar idea, and perhaps it belongs to poetry rather than science. So does the other form of orgone energy which Reich called DOR because it is destructive. It is this energy which is used to repress the normal sexual urge.

The concept is easier to grasp if we consider the comparable case of Freud's binary classification of instincts under *Eros* and *Thanatos*. DOR is similar to *Thanatos* (Death). Just as Freud pictured aggression being turned inward against the Self and resulting in repression, so DOR is "sequestered" from creative orgone and then turns against it. However, the analogy breaks down because DOR is not so powerful as creative orgone. In the long run the forces of destruction and life-negation will be overcome by love. It is reminiscent of the ancient religion of Persia which taught that there were two immeasurably powerful cosmic beings, the principle of light and the principle of darkness, Good pitted against Evil, God against the Devil.

The Master Formula

In this science or mythology, Reich believed he had found positive proof of the existence of orgone. He claimed that anyone could *see* orgone in his laboratory. It had a blue colour. In its creative form orgone was love; consequently love was a material substance. If this sounds odd, something of the sort is implicit in any view of the mind–body relation which affirms their identity. Unless mind is an immaterial substance it must be a material substance. Thoughts and feelings must be capable of being translated into perceptible activities of the brain and nervous system.

Reich was driven to what seems a rather fantastic extreme by the passion to unify his experience and reduce it to a master formula. As a young man he was fascinated by Henri Bergson's philosophy of creative evolution. Its ruling idea was the *élan vital*, a teleological urge within all living organisms from which Bernard Shaw's Life Force is derived. "For some time I was taken for a 'crazy Bergsonian' because I agreed with him in principle, without, however, being able to state exactly where his theory left a gap", he wrote. "There was no denying the principle of a creative power governing life; only it was not satisfactory as long as it was not tangible, as long as it could not be described or practically handled. For, rightly, this was considered the supreme goal of natural science. The vitalists seemed to come closer to our understanding of the life principle than the mechanists who dissected life before trying to understand it." (*The Function of the Orgasm*, p. 46.)

It was impossible to be both a vitalist and a mechanist. For long Reich was torn between these polar opposites until illumination finally came. Man was not merely a machine, nor was he impelled by some mysterious 'entelechy' as Driesch held. The motive power of man and everything else in the universe, animate or inanimate, is a hitherto undiscovered form of energy.

Mobile orgone could be precipitated into the bions he claimed to have observed electroscopically and by means of Geiger-Müller counters. Their pulsation was governed by the same formula as orgasm : viz., mechanical tensions → bio-electric charge → bio-electric discharge → mechanical relaxation. This leads Reich to the curious idea that the tension followed by discharge in orgasm corresponds to bio-energetic processes throughout all Nature. For what is discharged by both partners in the sex act is orgone, and orgone is "functionally identical" with love.

Reich not only attempted to reach a synthesis of the opposites of vitalism and mechanism, he laid the basis of a Nature-Mysticism. In view of his avowed hostility to mysticism, it seems surprising that he should develop in this direction. The intensified persecution of the last years undoubtedly affected his mental balance. In his book *The Murder of Christ* he identified himself with Christ. While in prison he attended some church services and wrote in a letter to his son : "I was deeply moved; I felt a new, universal faith in Life and Love, comprising monotheistic beliefs, races, etc., is becoming a dire necessity to counterweight the 'Enemy of Man'." In her biography of Reich his wife admitted that she had not been able to understand this development as it seemed so far removed from his thinking as she had known it.

Sex and Civilization

The mainstream of his thinking is what concerns us here. The concept of "psychic energy" was central before it became identified with orgone. Although it may not be synonymous with sexual energy, the lack of attention paid to other forms makes it seem almost so. The major human problem, according to Reich, is that sexual energy is denied spontaneous release in most civilized people. The consequences of this energy being dammed are widespread and darken social life like a plague. All anti-social behaviour springs from secondary drives which are due to "a disturbance of the natural capacity for love". What love means apart from orgasm is not clear.

At first sight Reich's ideas may seem much the same as Freud's, but Freud had a broader view of the sexual instinct. Its importance for civilized communities lay in the capacity to direct it to an aim remote from sexual gratification. This is not necessarily the neurotic result that Reich deplores. Freud's attitude to sex has often been travestied, but he expresses it quite plainly : "The nature of my extension of the concept of sexuality is of a two-fold kind. (1) Sexuality is divorced from its too close connection with the genitals and is regarded as a more comprehensive bodily function having pleasure as its goal and only secondarily coming to serve the ends of reproduction. (2) The sexual impulses are regarded as including all those merely affectionate and friendly impulses to which usage applies the exceedingly ambiguous word 'Love'." (*An Autobiographical Study,* p. 927.)

The ambiguity of the word is not lessened by burying it under an even vaguer term like *Eros.* Freud regarded some diversion of genital sex as a necessity of civilized life, not as a form of neurosis. Neuroses may arise, of course, but without repression he thinks we should be living in a state of primitive barbarism. He writes : "One gets the impression that culture is something which was imposed by a minority that understood how to possess itself of power and coercion." Whereas Freud regards this as part of the inescapable human predicament, since "all men are destructive" and anti-social tendencies predominate, Reich rejects the conclusion that life must always follow this tragic pattern. True, a cultivated minority have imposed their will in the past, and feathered their own nests at the same time, but there is no biological reason why such a state of affairs should be perpetuated. Taboos on sex are sociological, not biological. A social revolution could eliminate them. There is no reason to suppose

91

that the quality of culture need suffer, though it would be different, nearer to anarchy than despotism.

On this issue I think that the majority of informed opinion today would agree with Reich that we need not regard ourselves as doomed by an innate destructiveness. If Freud had looked more closely at the animal kingdom, he would have found no evidence of purposeless destruction. It is not even true that man is the only animal to fight his own species. Like other herd animals, man fights to preserve territorial claims, but the predators are other groups within the same species. Thus wolves, with whom Hobbes cynically compared men, will fight a member of their own pack, but rarely to the death, and usually because of sexual rivalry. The combat is more serious if there is an attack by another pack.

Ethology is a fairly recent study. N. Tinbergen even doubts if there is a general aggressive instinct among animals. In spite of the blood-stained record of human history, Man has the same instinctive reluctance to kill his enemy as those animals who stop short of the final lethal blow. If it were not for the development of long-range weapons this would be more evident. The point is so relevant to contemporary problems that Tinbergen is worth quoting: "The same restrictive inhibition of the fighting drive is found in man. One reason why wholesale slaughter in modern warfare is relatively easily accomplished is to be found in the modern long-range arms that prevent one witnessing the action of lethal weapons. Our instinctive reluctance to kill is strengthened by the sight of a dying man in a multilated condition. Hence one is much less reluctant to direct artillery fire at a distant tower, thereby killing the enemy artillery observer, than to cut his throat in a man-to-man fight. Our instinctive disposition has not changed with the rapid development of mechanical long-range killing apparatus." (*The Study of Instinct*, by N. Tinbergen, O.U.P., 1951, p. 209.)

The Wheat and the Chaff

When one looks back across the years at the early days of the psychoanalytical movement, it is only to be expected that some theories have had to be modified and others scrapped. So many of Freud's seminal ideas have been incorporated in the modern outlook that we easily forget that he was a Victorian and very much a child of his time. Some of his ideas have been superseded by later developments in psychology. His account of unconscious mechanisms largely stands, but his one-time concept of a Death Instinct, against which Reich so strongly protests, has few adherents. If many of Reich's ideas have also failed to survive, even apart from the more fanciful flights of his last period, some are of great interest to a young generation turning their backs on tradition and authority. To a generation disillusioned by Soviet Communism and scornful of the Capitalist Establishment Reich's attempt to reconcile Marx and Freud is particularly meaningful.

Reich's optimism is stimulating, but there are important areas of life left out of his scheme. It cannot be true that people are submissive solely because of the suppression of their infantile sexuality. They are not as docile as all that. We simply do not know whether students demonstrating in the campus were slapped down for masturbating as infants or given complete freedom. It is all left to guesswork. But we do know a great deal more about the first year of life than Reich and his fellow analysts did forty years ago. The seeds of future neurosis can be sown by a faulty child–mother relationship quite remote from anything connected with sex.

A bad mother may not take the trouble to punish infantile masturbation. She leaves the child to its own devices and certainly cannot be bothered with toilet training and feeding by the clock. There is no question then of the heavy hand of parental authority. The child has plenty of freedom—but insufficient affection.

Today the need of the child for frequent close contact with the mother is widely recognized. If this non-verbal communication is regarded as a nascent sexuality the word is so all-embracing that it is practically meaningless. But there is no reason to suppose that the longing to lie safely in the arms of the mother has anything to do with sex. It may originate in what is sometimes called separation anxiety.

93

We do not know what deep-seated traces are left by the original separation from the body of the mother. Otto Rank coined the term "trauma of birth". Unfortunately, like Reich, he made the mistake of trying to reduce all neuroses to a single cause, the primal anxiety of separation from the mother. The idea is taken to somewhat extravagant lengths by Nandon Fodon, but it was explored more moderately by Ian Suttie in a highly original study, *The Origins of Love and Hate*, first published in 1935. He advanced a very persuasive answer to the question of why the child is so afraid of losing the mother. Everyone knows how a child cries when the mother leaves it, even for a short time. John Bowlby has shown that a real psychic injury may be inflicted by prolonged absence, as when children were evacuated from London in the Second World War. The younger they are the more harm is done, though it may not be apparent for many years. The anxiety is nothing more than a fear of loneliness. An infant cannot tell whether he will be left alone for a short time or whether he has been completely abandoned. His response is instinctive, the instinct of self-preservation.

The mother gives him a sense of security which is vital if emotional growth is not to be stunted from the start. Just as the growing body may suffer from a deficiency disease, so the psyche may also be warped by emotional malnutrition. The thwarting of the hunger for love, which is the need to feel safe, may give rise to anti-social behaviour when the child is older. The dread of loneliness is really a desire to be with other people, to matter very much to some of them.

It is easy to see how this can lead to a sense of social responsibility. Among the higher animals those who are social nurture their young, and this in turn makes them gregarious. Sociability seems like a continuation of dependence on the nurturing parent long after the actual need for the mother is outgrown. But it is not a component of sexuality. The instinct of self-preservation is prior to sex and even more fundamental than reproduction of the species, for if the individual lacked this instinct there would be no possibility of reproduction. The species would become extinct.

Anxiety in an infant cannot be due to sexual frustration. It is the response to the imagined loss of love, since only the awareness of being loved enables the infant to feel safe. When he is not given love he is angry, but this is merely an intensification of the separation anxiety. There is no necessity to think of aggression as being an independent biological instinct. It serves the purpose of self-preservation in some circumstances.

The energy of aggression, like sexual energy, is part of the total energy system of the organism. It is misleading to speak of sexual energy or aggressive energy as though they were in separate compartments. The organism uses its available energy for organic maintenance and development. This is why from the moment of birth an infant needs physical reassurance in the mother's arms or at the breast. When he is held close to the mother's body the total union which was severed when he left the womb seems partly restored. The contact with the mother's skin not only gives a feeling of security, it is an unusually pleasant sensation in its own right. The value of tactile stimulation is coming to be recognized more widely.

Tactile Deprivation

Ashley Montagu cites the findings of other anthropologists in very different cultures. Observations in Africa, the South Seas and South America suggest that when children are given tactile stimulation they are not driven to use such substitutes for the mother as thumb-sucking. In the Canadian Arctic an Eskimo mother carries her infant on her back, next to her skin. It defecates and urinates in that position and she cheerfully cleans it; and she swings it round to the breast when it wants to be fed. The result of this happy, uninhibited intimacy is the formation of a well-regulated, altruistic personality.

Anna Freud has pointed out that it is a primitive need of the child to have a close and warm contact with another person's body before sleeping, but we frown upon this in our own type of society. "The infant's biological need for the care-taking adult's

95

constant presence is disregarded in our western culture, and children are exposed to long hours of solitude owing to the misconception that it is healthy for the young to sleep, rest, and later play alone." (*Normality and Pathology in Childhood*, International Universities Press, N.Y. 1965, p. 155.)

And what happens in later life to children deprived of this "primitive need"? The men are usually clumsy in their approaches to sex and wholly lacking in finesse. They have never been initiated into the subtleties of body language. They have been taught to regard tenderness as unmanly and to shrink from all outward demonstrativeness. They probably find it very difficult to say the words "I love you", though this is just what their partner is longing to hear. The trouble is that they have not experienced the expression of mother-love in non-verbal terms.

A woman who has been denied the intimacy of skin contacts in infancy is likely to feel a revulsion at the thought of exposing her body to an adult. The fact that such intimacy was avoided by her parents seems to imply that it is either wrong or merely disgusting. On the other hand, some women have confessed that they enticed more men to have intercourse because it would satisfy their desire to be held and cuddled. Dr. Alexander Lowen, a disciple of Reich, published a number of case histories of women who suffered a lack of tactile stimulation in infancy and subsequently engaged in sexual activities in a desperate attempt to gain bodily contact. "This compulsive activity may give the impression that these persons are over-sexed", writes Lowen. "They are, if anything, under-sexed, for the activity stems from a need for erotic stimulation rather than from a feeling of sexual charge or excitement."

Ashley Montagu takes this quotation from *The Betrayal of the Body* and makes the following significant comment: "These are important points, for they draw attention to the fact that in the Western world it is highly probable that sexual activity, indeed the frenetic preoccupation with sex that characterizes Western culture, is in many cases not the expression of sexual interest at all, but rather a search for the satisfaction of the need for contact." (*Touching: The Human Significance of the Skin*, Columbia University Press, 1971, p. 167.)

Reich would say that such a search is plainly neurotic and that the undischarged libido is seeking a substitute for orgasm. But does this explain the admission by a former call-girl to an American psychiatrist, "In a way I used sex to be held"? Dr. Marc H. Hollender, of the University of Pennsylvania, made a study of thirty-nine women, mostly suffering from depression, and found that the need for body contact varied with individuals. With some it was compulsive and not easy to satisfy, unlike oral needs which can be consoled by drinking or smoking at times of stress.

We seem here to be dealing with a biological need which is not confined to the human species. Although body contacts are kept to a a minimum in some cultures, notably our own, it would be a mistake to suppose that what is suppressed is thereby eliminated. So far from uprooting the desire for body contacts the characteristically English taboo on tenderness and cult of the stiff upper lip has provoked a backlash. The pendulum has swung against the Spartan upbringing of children, especially in regard to their feeding and toilet habits. The more relaxed attitude may be partly due to the growth of permissiveness, but it is not directly connected with sex. The body and its functions no longer inspire a sense of shame. More and more people have learned to look on nakedness without guilt and with the naturalness found in a nudist camp. The pleasure of looking at the naked body (*skoptophilia*) and the equally primitive pleasure of touching are more than a prelude to sexual relations.

The recent growth of groups variously described as "Encounter" or "Sensitivity Training" is further evidence of the old barriers to bodily communication breaking down. In these groups the members are encouraged to hold hands, embrace and sometimes bathe together in the nude. The scandal that such defiance of conventions arouses is only to be expected. There are the usual dark whispers of nameless orgies, but they have no foundation in a properly organized group.

A more sophisticated line of criticism is that the craving for body contacts is a regression to childhood. Any psychiatrist who

97

makes this charge is usurping the function of the priest and proclaiming the new sin of immaturity in place of the old sin of immorality. It is obvious that some kinds of infantile behaviour would be decidedly unwholesome if carried forward into adult life. Fixation on the mother when charged with sexuality becomes incestuous. Yet, with another woman, a continuation of such infantile gratifications as skin-to-skin contact are entirely innocuous. In situations of stress there is a certain relief in the bodily and oral satisfactions surviving in one form or another from infancy, e.g. the consoling embrace, drinking, smoking, etc.

Having crusaded for the best part of my professional life for greater sexual freedom, I am the last person to denigrate sex. My own clinical experience, however, compels me to join issue with Reich's extreme emphasis on the importance of a particular type of orgasm. I do not think that all physical contacts—kissing, stroking, embracing—should be dismissed as meaningless or as a neurotic subterfuge unless they are deliberately directed towards intercourse. The infant who gets security from feeling the body of his mother is motivated by the instinct of self-preservation. This evokes a variety of activities which run parallel with the sexual drive. They may or may not merge together but they derive from a different source.

9 Freud and Reich Revalued

Psychoanalysis looks to early infancy for the origin of neuroses. The relationship of the child to the mother is crucial. Various stages of development are enumerated and at any of these growth may be arrested. There are so many difficult hurdles that it seems scarcely less than a miracle that anyone survives unscathed. Freud regarded these successive stages primarily as manifestations of sexuality. This was the most original and distinctive contribution made by Freud seventy years ago, and as there had been hardly even a mention of sex in what passed for psychology at that time the effect was electrifying.

Among the group of doctors that collected around Freud was Alfred Adler, who subsequently defected and followed an independent line. He was not convinced of the necessity of probing far back into childhood to understand a patient's problems. He concluded that more often than not the problems were not sexual at all. They were due to disappointed ambition, failure to gain adequate recognition, the humiliation of some physical abnormality such as a club foot, obesity, a stammer. This gave a sense of inferiority which could be depressing, though often it acted as a spur. It was a mistake to think that everybody with an "inferiority complex" is necessarily a timid, submissive sort of person. On the contrary, he may be boastful and arrogant, giving the impression that he is convinced of his own superiority. He compensates for his deficiency by putting on a bluff.

We all come across such examples, though the credit goes to Adler for stripping off the disguises—the short, insignificant-looking man who becomes bumptious to redress the balance, the semi-impotent man who boasts of his sexual prowess. All this strikes the layman as sound common sense. The language Adler uses is free from jargon and very different from the technical vocabulary of psychoanalysis. It may be that this is one reason why his contribution has not received the professional recognition it deserves.

After Adler's important early study of the psychological effect of organ inferiority he turned to popularization and some of the phrases he coined have passed into everyday speech. He also influenced the thinking of such neo-Freudians as Karen Horney and Ian Suttie. But they regard the desire for power as only one among several possible neurotic traits, and as a sign of the failure to obtain love. The individual feels that if people do not love him he can at least force them to notice him and perhaps admire him.

I think Adler fell into the trap that has ensnared many scientists, not only psychologists. He thought he had found the *one* cause of all neuroses. "Every neurosis can be understood as an attempt to free oneself from a feeling of inferiority in order to gain a feeling of superiority", he wrote. Reich made a similar pronouncement about sexual failure. The truth is that for some people power and prestige are more important than sexual gratification, whereas for others the reverse is the case. Any psychological principle that is not riddled with exceptions must be suspect.

The Meaning of Life

After his break with Freud and the founding of Individual Psychology, as Adler called his system, he placed more and more emphasis on the importance of a sense of social responsibility in maintaining individual mental health. He found that everyone devises his own style of life to suit what seem to be his needs. This pattern is the *meaning* he gives to his life. If he is sexually inadequate, withdrawn, unable to make friends, what Life means to him is the ability to shield himself against hurt, to escape from difficult situations untouched. Another type of man who faces all problems with courage, whose love-life is satisfying, and who takes part in various social tasks, gives a different meaning to his life. Instead of being isolated on a narrow ledge of egoism, he goes out to meet his fellows to form new creative relationships, to co-operate in social enterprises.

As Adler expresses it: "All failures—neurotics, criminals, drunkards, problem children, suicides, perverts and prostitutes—are failures because they are lacking in fellow-feeling and social interest. They approach the problems of occupation, friendship and sex without the confidence that they can be solved by co-operation. The meaning they give to life is a private meaning; no one else is benefited by the achievment of their aims and their interest stops short at their own persons. Their goal of success is a goal of mere fictitious personal superiority and their triumphs have meaning only to themselves . . . Every human being strives for significance; but people always make mistakes if they do not see that their whole significance must consist in their contribution to the lives of others." (*What Life should Mean to You* by Alfred Adler, Unwin Books, 1962, p. 12.)

To the purist it is impermissible to mix science with ethics in this way. Freud insisted that the analyst should be strictly neutral and avoid giving advice. Neither politics nor morality had any place in the psychoanalytical consulting-room. But the urgent problems of life cannot be so easily excluded. As Aristotle pointed out over 2,000 years ago, man is a political animal. His psychological health depends as much on his participation in the life of the community as on his sexual capacity. There is no sense in asking which is the more important because both are necessary if we are to realize our full potential.

No Universal Formula

In my own experience it is virtually impossible not to give advice at times, if only by implication. The patient comes because he needs help. And once he has explained his problem, which may not be the real problem, the question arises to which category he belongs. How easy it would be if, following Reich, we gave all our attention to his sexual difficulties; or, following Adler, we concentrated solely on his life style; or, following other mentors, we decided that he suffered from lack of affection. There are many more pigeon-holes in which to place the case history. Sometimes I have found it best to forget all about these conflicting theories.

There are people who can undoubtedly be labelled with fair accuracy; but others resist all attempts to classify them. They are all individuals with unique backgrounds no matter how they resemble each other superficially. There is no simple recipe, no universally applicable formula, because we do not yet know enough about human behaviour, which is even more complex and intractable than the behaviour of the atom. It seems to me that in our present state of knowledge the right attitude must be eclectic, making use as the circumstances dictate of the insights that seem most appropriate.

The armchair psychologist constructs a system that is perfectly logical and completely self-consistent—qualities that are conspicuously lacking in real life. The ideal of perfect mental health is useful as a pointer to the direction we ought to go, but it is not a goal which anyone is likely to reach. If too much emphasis is given to it our efforts may be counter-productive. People will start worrying about all the ways, however trivial, in which they fall short of an impossibly high standard.

A great deal of harm has already been done by paying disproportionate attention to sexual orgasm. I have always insisted that what matters most about sex is that it is enjoyed. If people are told that this is not good enough, and that sex must be enjoyed in a special way, the simple satisfaction they once experienced may be spoilt. The mere idea that they have been missing something essential in their love-making makes them self-conscious and so is self-defeating. It may well be true that sexual satisfaction can be made more intense by a course of Reich's vegetotherapy. The number of people who can undergo the treatment is minimal. The number who become dissatisfied because they have heard about it and cannot be treated is much larger. Moreover it is not enough for *one* partner to be orgastically potent unless the other is able to co-operate. We must not confuse love with love-making!

The Mechanics of Sex

This is not to say that Reich's plea for uninhibited sexual surrender is based on a mistake. Where I think he is at fault is in laying too much stress on the mechanism of orgasm. The same can be said of Kinsey and of the experiments of Masters and Johnson. All these investigations provide valuable information about the physiology of sex. Their weakness is in coming close to the fallacy of reductionism, i.e. the interpretation of behaviour at a higher level of organization in terms of a lower level. For example, it is true that man is composed of atoms and molecules, but to describe his activities in these terms only would be like Hamlet without the Prince of Denmark.

Dr. Alexander Lowen, a former student of Wilhelm Reich, makes this kind of criticism of both Kinsey and Masters and Johnson. He strongly repudiates the latter's statement that "the human female's physiologic responses to affective sexual stimulation develop with consistency regardless of the source of the psychic or physical sexual stimulation". Since under laboratory conditions it was demonstrated that orgasm and even multiple orgasm could be produced in women by means of a vibrator, it is difficult to see where this differs from the type of orgasm described by Reich.

According to Lowen : "If we ignore the factors that determine feeling and emotional response, we lose sight of the human and spiritual qualities that make life meaningful. The great importance of the sexual function for human happiness requires that it be studied in terms of its emotional significance and not as a mechanical or physiological act of release." (*Love and Orgasm*, Signet Books, 1965, p. 237.) That seems entirely reasonable, but Reich's tremendous emphasis on abolishing muscular rigidity and bringing a "dead pelvis" to life is more of a mechanical than an emotional approach. A tenderly loving relationship is not absolutely necessary for orgastic response if, as Reich says, this may be no more than a brief encounter.

It may be there is a lack of clarity in translating Reich's words from German, but there is no question that he devotes vastly more space to the physiological than to the emotional manifestations of sex. He gives the impression, rightly or wrongly, that love is an aid to orgasm rather than that orgasm is an expression of love. Dr. Lowen must be acquitted of this error. He refuses to base the phenomenon of orgasm on physical facts alone. The special feeling of tenderness in a caress, as distinct from other forms of tactile stimulation, gives it a special quality.

This is true enough. It does not follow that the genital reflex caused by mechanical or other means is not a genuine orgasm. Lowen grudgingly admits that it is possible, though not probable, to have a vaginal orgasm through clitoral stimulation. But whatever criticisms may be made of the Masters and Johnson experiments they do seem to have proved conclusively that there is only one orgasm, not a choice between clitoral or vaginal reflexes. No doubt a sexual relationship is richer and more satisfying when the partners have a deep mutual affection, but the reflex movements which involve the whole body at the sexual climax are no different. They can be induced by masturbation or even by passionate kissing.

Most people who come to an analyst or psychotherapist because of sexual difficulties may benefit in varying degrees, though some conditions can actually be made worse by expecting too much. The hopeless search for the perfect orgasm is only one example. Yet another is the anxious effort to suppress anything which they have been told is "immature". I am not aware of any agreed definition of maturity, but the idea that we should eliminate most forms of behaviour that originate in infancy leads to absurdities. I have already referred to the importance of body contacts, but some psychologists go so far as to say that hot baths are a regression to pre-natal existence in the womb. The water is compared to the amniotic fluid, the plug to the cervix, emergence from the bath to birth. Even if this were the case, what of it? Must emotionally mature people stop having baths?

The first impact of the hard world, after the Nirvana-like peace of the womb, leaves a trace that is never cmpletely lost. The same is true of all impressions made in the most plastic period of our lives. They remain a part of us like the early rings of a tree which are added with age but are never obliterated. The effect of environment is passed on as much as heredity is transmitted. Everything we have experienced is built into our personality like the strokes of an artist's brush on canvas. But we are the artist who fashions what we become—the character that is always in the making and never finished.

The Fight for Freedom

Reflection on the ideas of Wilhelm Reich has led me to take a hard look at some things I may have taken too much for granted. I have long been a champion of a liberal attitude to sexual morality. Some of the battles in which I took part have been won—homosexual law reform, obscene publications reform, abortion law reform, to name a few. That they were all mainly concerned with bringing about a more rational and humane attitude to sex does not mean that there are no other major problems. I may have given the impression of being too pre-occupied with sex, but that is probably due to the intensity of the opposition to an open discussion of the subject. In 1942 I stood in the dock of the Old Bailey charged with publishing "an obscene libel", which was the curious technical phrase applied to my book *Love without Fear*. I insisted on trial by jury and was acquitted. Had I been found guilty the penalties would have been heavy, including possible professional ruin. My offence was to state in language that the ordinary man and woman could understand what others had published with impunity because they took refuge in Latin terms and medical jargon. Against such a background of prejudice and hostility it was inevitable that sex should be seen somewhat out of focus.

There had been some advance since Charles Bradlaugh stood in the same dock at the Central Criminal Court sixty-five years earlier, arraigned for publishing a book on birth control in plain English at a price that the working-class reader who needed it most could afford. But in the past thirty years the change in public attitudes as well as the law has accelerated. We have witnessed the beginning of the sexual revolution which Reich preached but did not live to see. Almost anything except hard-core pornography can now be published and sold openly. Yet on the dust-cover of the first edition of *Love without Fear* it had been necessary to state: "The author has written this book for those who are married or about to be married, and in this connection the booksellers' co-operation is requested." We may well smile when even homosexual themes have become common in novels, films and on television. Full frontal nudity and simulated intercourse can be seen on the stage. A Jugoslav film on Reich entitled *"WR—Mysteries of the Organism"* had a good run in London and was highly praised by the critics. No one seemed troubled because in one scene it showed a girl making a plaster cast of her boy-friend's erect penis.

It is not so much a question today of whether permissiveness has gone far enough, but rather whether the concentration on sexual problems has distracted too much attention from equally urgent problems. Reich believed that sexual liberation should go hand in hand with an economic revolution. As the practical possibility of achieving a socialist society seemed more and more remote, except at the cost of the very authoritarianism he abhorred, he pinned his hopes on the more limited target of changing individual attitudes. But he still held that sexual frustration was the major social malaise, more destructive of happiness than economic hardship. He seemed to feel with D. H. Lawrence that if only people led satisfying sexual lives, all other problems would gradually be solved or seem less important.

Unfortunately there are no grounds for this optimism. Eminent scientists are warning us that the world is doomed unless the population explosion is halted and the pollution of air, sea and land stopped. The sudden interest in the hitherto neglected science of ecology is a measure of the alarm. And if all these fears were removed, we should still have the threat of a nuclear holocaust hanging over the world. We say much less about this nowadays because we try to tell ourselves that none of the Great Powers would invite its own destruction. This may be so, but the anxiety remains even if it is thrust below the level of consciousness. How could it be seriously maintained with problems of this magnitude facing the world that the chief source of neurotic anxiety is sexual? What of the victims of race prejudice, or of a ruthlessly competitive economic system, or of the alienation of the mass of workers in an increasingly mechanized society? Perhaps many of these problems could be ameliorated by greater sexual satisfactions, but I doubt if this, by itself, would provide the solution. It is to Reich's credit that he recognized the damaging consequences of such a distorting environment on the individual. But today the patriarchal family appears to be on the way out. Discipline of any kind is becoming a dirty word. Parents and teachers spare the rod, and they do not thereby spoil the child. Among students there is even less submission to authority. None of them nowadays would regard the function of the university to be *in loco parentis*. Compared with earlier generations, young people today have been "liberated". But it is not only sexual freedom that they want. Many are passionately concerned about social justice, hence the "demos" and the stormy scenes on the campus. In the United States particularly they often baffle their elders by turning their backs on the American way of life and its materialistic values. Such social phenomena have taken most people by surprise and force us to reconsider some of the assumptions that have been too uncritically accepted by many psychologists.

Instinct and Environment

Two of the most doubtful assumptions of Freudian theory were named by Reich as "biologism" and "atomism". Biologism means that the drives governing human behaviour are thought to be innate. The alternative view is that human behaviour is largely conditioned by environment. Obviously no one would deny that we are born with powerful instincts, but how these instincts operate is determined by the type of society in which we are brought up. Leaving aside the vexed question of whether aggression is an instinct, there can be no doubt that people behave with different degrees of aggressiveness. Anthropologists cite examples of societies in which the members are conditioned to be pacific and co-operative, whereas others are fiercely combative and interested only in self-aggrandizement. There is striking evidence that the type to which a child will belong depends far more on his early relationship with his parents than on biological drives.

One cannot fail to be impressed by the utterly different patterns of culture found among South Sea peoples living often within no great distance of one another. For example, the Mundugumor of New Guinea detest rearing children and bring them up to be quarrelsome and warlike. They have developed a Hobbesian type of social organization in which every man's hand is

107

against every other man. But the gentle Arapesh lavish affection on their children, and although they are desperately poor they help their neighbours without thought of reward.

There are many such examples showing the utter inadequacy of a purely biological approach, either in regard to sexual relationships or wider forms of social behaviour. The importance of this evidence is that it disposes of the theory that man is incurably aggressive, and that brutality and war are the inevitable outcome of human nature. If brutality and war are simply the function of a certain social order, they can be eliminated by changing the social order. It is always difficult to change the structure of society, but it is not impossible. Society is made by man, and what man can make he can change. Instead of Freudian pessimism about the function of civilization we have reasons for hope if there are no biological obstacles to man's ability to shape his own destiny.

Closely associated with biological determinism is the equally fallacious "atomization" at which Reich protested. All schools of psychology which treat the individual in isolation from his environment come under this criticism. The patient's problem is viewed as an internal conflict to which the social background is no more relevant than it would be to some physiological disorder.

The psychosomatic approach abolishes the old, misleading distinction between mind and body, but it does not go far enough. We must also cease to think of the individual as an encapsulated nomad in the social structure. The unfolding of consciousness from the moment of birth is not a phenomenon that can be understood as though it took place solely within the circle of family relationships. The family itself is set within a wider background. The influences to which the family is exposed are passed on to the growing child and help to form his mental attitudes. It is not just a matter of the Id being kept under control by the reality-thinking of the ego and the moralism of the Super-ego. The customs and ideals of society are a matrix in which the child's consciousness is formed.

Infantile Sexuality

I have become increasingly sceptical of the usefulness of the concept of infantile sexuality. The more the meaning of "sexuality" is watered down, because it is obviously absurd to suppose that an infant can have sexual feelings in any ordinary sense, the less fruitful the idea becomes. I know that orthodox Freudians are indignant at any suggestion that "sexual" means what most people might suppose. Yet they themselves describe the child's jealous love of his mother as an "Oedipus situation", and Oedipus, in the Greek drama, committed incest by marrying his mother in a perfectly unambiguous way. The use of such a term by Freud is loaded with associations that may not be intended, though they might have been expected. A similar semantic confusion arises from the use of the term masturbation to describe an infant's genital manipulation. This is very different from masturbation at puberty. To use the same word invites confusion.

Parents may make an unnecessary fuss about the incipient sexuality which they notice in the child, and which is often no more than curiosity to discover new sources of sensation. Oral gratification—sucking, feeding, at the breast or with a substitute —is probably more intense. But curiosity is one of the most powerful motivations in a human being, a fact that was recognized in ancient mythology thousands of years before psychology began. It was curiosity, not sexual desire, that made Eve pluck the forbidden fruit. And it was curiosity that made Pandora, in the Greek myth, open a box she had been prohibited to touch. The long history of man's inventions from the Stone Age to the rise of modern Science is the outcome of the restless urge to explore the unknown.

The Freudian theory that the search for knowledge began with sexual curiosity seems to me a typical example of an attempt to reduce almost all drives to sex. It seems far more likely that the prehistoric hunter who first made a knife from flint, and the first artist who painted figures on the walls of a cave, were both satisfying an impulse to get *power* over the material—an impulse

109

that has culminated in harnessing the energy of the atom and kindling a fire as fierce as the sun itself.

The genius of Freud towers like a giant above his successors, but that does not diminish the value of their contributions, any more than it implies that no substantial change need ever be made in the original formulation. Freud inspired a body of brilliant fellow-workers, some of whom finally broke away to follow their own trails. Adler, Jung, Stekel, Reich, Fromm are among the deviationists whose ideas nevertheless had their roots in the revolutionary changes ushered in by Freud.

Reich Revalued

As a psychiatric clinician faced continually by human problems which do not fit neatly into any rigid theory, I take whichever insight seems likely to be most helpful. There are some individuals whose behaviour can best be understood in terms of power, others who are clearly suffering from sexual frustration. Reich's technique of character-analysis may prove to be his most important single contribution. It has received far less publicity than his orgone theory and has suffered unfairly by association with the latter. An interesting tribute is paid by Professor Paul Edwards in a long and sympathetic article in *The Encyclopedia of Philosophy* (Macmillan & Co. and The Free Press, New York): "Philosophically the most interesting part of Reich's work is unquestionably what he calls the breakthrough into the vegetative realm, that is, his attempt to determine the physiological basis of neurotic phenomena." And he goes on: "During his early years in the United States, Reich did in fact find among his followers and sympathizers a number of remarkably talented men, from the most varied walks of life, who saw the dawn of a new enlightenment in his psychiatry and in the implications of his theories for education and for the proper direction of social reform. It would be difficult to convey to anybody who was not actually living in New York at that time the enthusiasm that was felt for Reich personally and for what were regarded as his liberating insights."

It is a mistake to think that Reich's reputation must stand

or fall with his theory of orgasm, and a further mistake to suppose that this theory, or any other, must be either entirely true or wholly false. I think the significance of orgasm is more complex than Reich allowed. There are other causes of neuroses besides sexual failure, and there are also some varieties of sexual satisfaction which cannot possibly be dismissed as failure because they do not conform to the prescribed pattern.

Fortunately Reich's achievement in psychiatry is wider than the theory of orgasm. It constitutes an innovation to the orthodox psychoanalytic treatment. He believed, for example, that it was not enough to remove the symptoms of which the patient complained, for although this might be superficially successful, the underlying character disturbance might continue and give rise to new symptoms.

The following appraisal by Dr. R. D. Laing, made four years ago, is a sign of awakened interest in Reich in serious professional circles and not only among the non-medical *avant-garde*: "Whether or not one agrees or disagrees with this or that of Reich's theory and practice, it is inescapable that he was a great clinician, with an unusually wide range. His accounts of his therapy with schizoid and schizophrenic patients will enlighten in some ways anyone involved in this enterprise. He understood the mess we are all in—hysteric, obsessional, psychosomatic, *homo-normalis*—as few have done. Yet one will look through a hundred journals in the Royal Society of Medicine without coming across one mention of him. Why is he never mentioned?" (*New Society*, March 1968).

The attempt to harmonize Marxism and psychoanalysis was not such a total failure as might appear on a cursory examination. They each contained elements that the other lacked: Marxism neglected the individual and psychoanalysis ignored the sociological factors. The possibility of a synthesis is one reason for the awakened interest in the line of thought started by Reich, if not in the details of his outlook. The social philosophy of Freud accepted the nineteenth-century view of human nature as instinctively aggressive and basically isolated, in need of strong leadership.

There cannot be many people today optimistic enough to

111

have faith in an *élite* which has "subordinated their instinctual life to the dictatorship of reason". Reich, on the other hand, rejected this authoritarianism. He believed that men were capable of a natural morality, provided they were not corrupted by the greed and violence of a ruthlessly competitive social system. Get rid of capitalism, stop repressing sexuality, and life will become joyous and spontaneous. You have nothing to lose but your inhibitions. This over-simplified message has an understandable appeal to a generation in revolt against the materialistic values of the acquisitive society, who take as their text "Make love not War".

Bibliography of American Editions

I. BOOKS BY REICH

Character Analysis. Carfango, Vincent R., tr. New York: Farrar, Straus and Giroux, 1972.

Ether, God and Devil and Cosmic Superimposition. (Illus.) Pol, Therese, tr. New York: Farrar, Straus and Giroux, 1972.

Function of the Orgasm. (Illus.) New York: Farrar, Straus and Giroux, 1961.

Invasion of Compulsory Sex-Morality. New York: Farrar, Straus and Giroux, 1971.

Listen, Little Man. (Illus.) New York: Farrar, Straus and Giroux, 1971.

Mass Psychology of Fascism. Carfango, Vincent R., tr. New York: Farrar, Straus and Giroux, 1970.

Murder of Christ: Emotional Plague of Mankind. New York: Farrar, Straus and Giroux, 1970.

Reich Speaks of Freud. Higgins, Mary and Raphael, Chester, eds.; Pol, Therese, tr. New York: Farrar, Straus and Giroux, 1967.

Selected Writings. (Illus.) New York: Farrar, Straus and Giroux, 1960.

Sex-Pol: Essays 1929–1934. Baxandall, Lee, ed. New York: Random House, 1972.

The Sexual Revolution. New York: Farrar, Straus and Giroux, 1963.

II. BOOKS AND ARTICLES REFERRED TO IN TEXT

Adler, Alfred. *What Life Should Mean to You.* New York: Putnam, 1959.

113

Brown, James A. *Freud and the Post-Freudians*. New York: Penguin, 1961.

Edwards, Paul, ed. *The Encyclopedia of Philosophy*. (8 vols.) New York: Macmillan, 1967.

Engels, Frederick. *The Origin of the Family*. New York: International Publishing Co., 1971.

Freud, Anna. *Normality and Pathology in Childhood: Assessments of Development*. New York: International Universities Press, 1966.

Freud, Sigmund. *An Autobiographical Study*. Strachey, James, ed. and tr. New York: Norton, 1963.

———. *An Outline of Psycho-Analysis*. Strachey, James, ed. and tr. New York: Norton, 1970.

Lowen, Dr. Alexander. *Love and Orgasm*. New York: New American Library, 1965.

Malinowski, Bronislaw. *The Sexual Life of Savages in North-Western Melanesia*. (Illus.) New York: Harcourt, Brace, Jovanovitch.

Masters, William H. and Johnson, Virginia E. *Human Sexual Response*. Boston: Little, Brown and Co., 1966.

Mead, Margaret. *Male and Female*: *A Study of the Sexes in a Changing World*. New York: Morrow, 1949.

Montagu, Ashley. *Touching*. New York: Columbia University Press, 1971.

Proceedings, American Philosopnical Society, No. 102, 1958, pp. 501–509.

Reich, Ilse Ollendorff. *Wilhelm Reich*: *A Personal Biography*. New York: St. Martin, 1969.

Rycroft, Charles, *Wilhelm Reich*. New York: Viking Press, 1972.

Tinbergen, N. *The Study of Instinct*. New York: Oxford University Press, 1969.